"Rusty speaks on one of the most importa[nt] grace, humor, and insight. Read it deepl[y] read it alone!"

—John Ortberg, Senior Pastor [...] [C]hurch, author of
I'd Like You More If You Were More Like Me

"Christianity was never meant to be a solo endeavor. In *Better Together*, Rusty George exposes the self-destructive folly of attempting to turn our personal relationship with the Lord into a private and isolated spiritual quest. It won't work. It never has."

—Larry Osborne, Pastor and author, North Coast Church

"If you are tired of languishing in loneliness, why not take steps toward connecting in community. Rusty's writing is honest and practical. His life and leadership model the message of *Better Together*."

—Dave Stone, Pastor, Southeast Christian Church

"As a professional athlete, I can tell you the value of community, teamwork, and playing together! Rusty's book captures what that can look like in everyday life!"

—Darryl Strawberry, Former Major League Baseball player,
Founder and Pastor of Strawberry Ministries

"What if your relationships were life-giving instead of draining? My friend Rusty George will get you there! His book *Better Together* overflows with practical wisdom."

—Lee Strobel, Bestselling author of *The Case for Christ*
and *The Case for Faith*

"The best leaders are ones who know how to work and collaborate with others. And *Better Together* can serve as a great resource for making sure you avoid isolation, and instead pursue building relationships that are life-giving and life-lasting."

—Brad Lomenick, Founder, BLINC, author of
H3 Leadership and *The Catalyst Leader*

"Rusty George writes with such conviction, humility, and laugh-out-loud humor, I'll read anything he writes. But this book hit a little too close to home. In a selfie world, we need this challenge that life truly is *Better Together*."

—Vince Antonucci, Pastor of Verve Church and
author of *God for the Rest of Us*

"Churches are famous for talking about community and infamous for not practicing it very well. Rusty offers a refreshing path to life-giving rather than draining relationships. It's his best book yet!"

—Gene Appel, Senior Pastor, Eastside Christian Church, Anaheim, CA

"Rusty helps us realize if you keep drifting toward isolation, one day you'll realize loneliness was not what you were seeking. *Better Together* helps right the course!"

—Dave Dummitt, Lead Pastor, 2/42 Community Church, Brighton, MI

"When Amazon can deliver in an hour, we are becoming increasingly more isolated as a people—if we so choose. Yet we were created for more. Rusty writes a much-needed, very timely book for our culture and church. This is a must-read for these days."

—Ron Edmondson, Pastor and author of *The Mythical Leader*

"*Better Together* gets at a problem we all face: How to have friends when we don't have time, or worse, don't have any interest!"

—Randy Frazee, Pastor and author of *The Connecting Church 2.0* and *Real Simplicity: Making Room for Life*

"*Better Together* gets at a problem we have always had, but it's so much harder now. I have less time and more things to do. Sometimes I just don't care enough, and I'm an extrovert! My friend Rusty (whom I do care about) will help you find a way to find balance and hopefully convince you that it's not too late to have, or be, a friend."

—Dr. Tim Harlow, Senior Pastor, Parkview Christian Church

"Few embrace and live out the idea of community like my friend Rusty George. In *Better Together*, Rusty guides us to see value in people and the strength that comes from doing life together."

—Caleb Kaltenbach, Author of *Messy Grace* and *God of Tomorrow*

"Some books I read silently to myself. *Better Together* I just had to read aloud to my wife. It is that good. It has to be shared!"

—Glen Keane, Disney Producer, Animator

"If you've been hurt by people (and who hasn't?) you probably resist people at some level. Rusty gets that. *Better Together* is a refreshingly honest look at community. Better yet, Rusty shows us how what initially hurt us can ultimately heal us."

—Carey Nieuwhof, Founding Pastor, Connexus Church

"In creation, God called a lot of things good. What's the first thing He said wasn't good? For man to be alone. Rusty George taps into that powerful truth in *Better Together* and communicates it deeply. It's worth your time and will help you find a life that keeps getting better."

—William Vanderbloemen, Founder and
CEO, Vanderbloemen Search Group

"As an introvert, I've justified isolation my entire life. In the pages you're about to read, Rusty confronted my greatest fears and best excuses, nudging me toward deeper friendship with others and with God."

—Jon Weece, Author of *Me Too*

"In his usual creative, insightful, and fun way, Rusty opens our eyes even further to our need for community. I've had the privilege of being in community with Rusty. He definitely practices what he preaches!"

—Mark Weigt, Lead Pastor, The Ridge Community Church

"Rusty not only reminds us that life is better connected, but shows us how we can make those connections more meaningful and catalytic."

—Bill Willits, Executive Director of Ministry
Environments, North Point Ministries

"*Better Together* gives practical guidance that addresses the resistance and fears people face in creating authentic, life-giving community. Every church with small groups needs this book."

—John Burke, Pastor and author of *No Perfect People
Allowed* and *Imagine Heaven*

"If you really want to go further faster, go together! Rusty's book *Better Together* will help you get there."

—Andy Stanley, Author, Communicator, and
Founder of North Point Ministries

Better Together

Better Together

DISCOVER THE POWER OF COMMUNITY

RUSTY GEORGE

BETHANYHOUSE

a division of Baker Publishing Group
Minneapolis, Minnesota

Published by Bethany House Publishers
11400 Hampshire Avenue South
Bloomington, Minnesota 55438
www.bethanyhouse.com

Bethany House Publishers is a division of
Baker Publishing Group, Grand Rapids, Michigan

Printed in the United States of America

Library of Congress Cataloging in Publication Control Number: 2017037364

ISBN 978-0-7642-3079-0

Cover design by Darren Welch Design

The author is represented by Don Gates from The Gates Group.

18 19 20 21 22 23 24   7 6 5 4 3 2 1

For my dad, Bob George.

The first extrovert I ever knew. While excruciating at times,
your enjoyment of people was my first lesson
that we truly are better together.

Contents

Foreword

The church saved my life. Well, to be accurate, God saved my life. But he used the people of a church to do it.

I grew up around church, but it wasn't until I was seventeen that I walked through the doors of a church on my own terms. I was wrestling with a four-year addiction and had a looming sense I was going to either go crazy, die, go to jail, or get some help.

Thankfully, I found my way to a small eclectic group of people in the church who met to encourage one another, learn and grow. They accepted me for who I was. They challenged and coached me. They prayed for me. They showed me what it looked like to face life's challenges with faith. Nobody in this group was super popular, cool, hip, or trendy. Nobody was perfect. And none of that mattered, because they loved me for me.

The church building, style of music, band, and teaching all played a part, but it was God using everyday people that made the difference. It is *always* God and people who make the greatest impact.

Since that experience, I've dedicated my life to helping others find hope and healing in God through the community of people called the church. I've seen my story repeated thousands of times as people experience life change in the context of relationships with others. I've witnessed marriages restored, destructive habits overcome, the freeing power of forgiveness, and the healing of hurts as strangers become friends with a common faith. I've learned that I need more than a *personal* relationship with Jesus, I need a *shared* relationship with Jesus. That shared relationship is where joy is maximized, hope is fueled, accountability is increased, and growth occurs. The shared relationship is where I'm able to find help facing my problems and offer help to others. Most important, it is where I realize I'm not alone.

Life is too hard to face alone. Nobody should have to sit in a hospital waiting room alone, or go through depression alone, or face the joys and challenges of parenting alone. Nobody should have to stand at the grave of a loved one alone. We need each other. And God has specifically placed communities of people, the church, to be that support network.

We can experience God in many ways. We can experience his presence in nature, music, the arts, work, or achievement. Yet none of these pathways comes close to how we can experience God's presence in community. It is people who are created in God's image. The most distraught, broken-down, hurting person is more beautiful than the most incredible ocean sunset or snow-covered mountain. Only people share the image of God. Sometimes people can drive us crazy, and often people are the problem. Yet in God's economy, people are also the solution.

This is what I love about *Better Together*. Rusty is a trusted voice that has not only helped untold numbers of individuals, but has done so with humility and grace. He's a rare leader with talent, character, and integrity. And he is a brilliant communicator, which comes through in his writing—brutally honest, hilarious, self-deprecating, insightful, and true. He points the way to what real friendship and community look like. He shows from his own life, and from the Bible, how we can learn and grow together.

We really are better together. Together we can laugh and cry, learn and love, persevere and endure. Together we can work to bring a little bit of heaven to earth for others. Together we can become the people God created us to be. *Better Together* shows us the way.

—Jud Wilhite, Senior Pastor of Central Church,
author of *Pursued*

Acknowledgments

Thank you . . .

To my first friends,
Scott Rigg, Steve Meyers, Mike Harenza, Shane Philip, and
Marc Glades.

To my friends I met in ministry,
Mark Weigt, Dave Dummit, Rob McDowell, T. D. Oakes, Mike
Breaux, Scott Hatfield, Chris Hahn, Brian Marshall, Justin
Moxley, Monte Wilkinson, Mike Hickerson, Caleb Kalten-
bauch, and Todd Elliot.

To my friends who made this book happen,
Andy McGuire, Jeanne Hedrick, Nancy Renich, and Bethany
House Publishers; Don Gates, Josh Komo, HiHat productions,
Jud Wilhite, and all my heroes who endorsed my book.

Acknowledgments

To my friends who make Real Life happen,
Fred Gray, Debbie Robert, Brennan Conklin, Daryn Teague,
Terry Meyer, Allen Meacham, Calvin Hedman, and the many
staff and countless volunteers who make Real Life Church what
it is!

To our friends who are family,
The Osborns, the Grays, and the Conklins.

To my family,
Mary, April, Tim, Rose, and Jerry.

To my favorite people in the world,
Lorrie, Lindsey, and Sidney. Together . . . you have made me
better.

Introduction

Taking a Selfie

We live in a selfie world.

Of course, what comes to mind are the pictures we take of ourselves with our smartphones. The phrase *Let me take a selfie* has become common language. In fact, I recently learned that the selfie stick has been outlawed at Disney parks due to how many people were getting injured as they inadvertently walked into them. We love to record our life and our position in it through photos.

When someone takes a selfie with you, whose image do you look at first? My bet is it's you! I know I do. When I'm involved in a group photo and have a chance to see it, I'm not looking at my friends or my gorgeous wife or my beautiful kids. I want to see how *I* look. Do I look old? Is my smile goofy? What about my midsection? (I'm working on it!)

Do you ever say, "Let's take another one" if it turned out badly? Or if it looks particularly flattering, do you say, "Hey, send me that one," thinking you'll post it on Facebook? I know I do. I don't consider myself a vain person, but if this pic is going on social media, I'd like to have some input. If it goes viral, I'd like to at least have my gut covered.

But the selfie world is not just about the stick or the pic. It's about our state of mind. We are consumed with ourselves—and encouraged to be. We live in a time when we have more health clubs, self-improvement regimens, life coaches, private tutors, personal trainers, and specialized therapists than ever before.

Think about all the things we are supposed to do to be a successful and thriving person: Exercise three times a week. Eat right. Journal. Work on your past. Plan for your future. Invest in your retirement. Set goals. Work hard. Build relationships. Always be learning something new. Oh, and try to relax.

Despite all these things, we are lonelier, more insecure, more depressed, and more anxious than ever before. You talk to friends. Read books. Seek counseling. Listen to mentors, experts, and life coaches. And the result is you still feel stuck. Shouldn't all the emphasis on self-improvement make you feel better?

Then you read the Bible, and it says you're supposed to "die to self." The way you do that is to bring every thought under subjection to Christ, allow His Spirit to manifest fruit in you, share your faith, renew your mind, forgive those who have wronged you, and so on. Sometimes I feel like I'm even more consumed with me when I'm so focused on trying to die to me. How do I die to myself when I'm constantly thinking about myself?

Author Henry Cloud quips, "The message of the church is often 'God is good, you are bad, so try harder.'"[1]

The result? Self-imposed guilt and self-imposed plans to make it right, which lead to more frustration and spiritual exhaustion.

Recently I found myself in such a place. It had been a particularly stressful few months filled with disappointments and unmet expectations, which heightened my anxiety. I often find that my life would be a lot easier if everyone (including God) would just do as I say.

In an effort to pull myself out of this funk, I dove deep into what some refer to as a self-hyphenated life: self-consumed and self-righteous for the sake of self-improvement. Now, as a pastor, I discourage this type of selfish behavior. But I pressed on, figuring if it would ultimately help my ministry, then surely the means could be justified.

It began with getting a counselor. I met regularly with a local therapist who would help me process my thoughts and give me some direction. Then I wondered if the problem was possibly medical. So I met with a psychiatrist to see if I needed medication. I scheduled an appointment with my doctor for a physical, my chiropractor for an adjustment, and even my dentist for a cleaning (you never know). I also worked on my physical health—I joined a gym, met with a trainer, downloaded diet apps, switched to bulletproof coffee,[2] counted carbs; I even took a shot of wheatgrass once in a while. While I did lower my cholesterol and raise my self-awareness, I still felt stuck.

It continued with lunch and phone calls with people I considered experts in the field. I met with pastors who had been in ministry longer than I had. I quizzed them on tricks of the trade and advice for longevity. I talked to business leaders who seemed to have mastered sustained success. I listened to podcasts from the wise and watched videos from experts. I read countless books on fear, anxiety, personal development, and meditation. While everything brought a small amount of relief, nothing seemed to last for long.

Even my daily devotions were focused on me. I read what I thought would help me. I picked devotionals promising to renew joy and facilitate closeness with God. I dusted off books from desert fathers or bought books from new pastors whose titles promised fuel for my soul. Still, something was missing.

Then one day I woke up and had a bit of a Solomon revelation: Meaningless, meaningless. . . . Everything is meaningless. In all of my work to fix myself, I had lost myself.

At the peak of my frustration, I found myself at lunch with a pastor who was visiting from out of town. I have tremendous respect for this leader and began to ask him my five or six questions about anxiety, fear, pain, and failure. Normally the responses I would get from others would be a few things to try or some encouraging pep talk, including words like "no pain, no gain" or "Jesus went to a cross . . . so get over it." But that day, I got a story.

He told me about a recent pain in his own life. Some longtime family friends had betrayed his trust, left his church, and ended their decade-long friendship. Their allegations were false, their offense was unjustified, but the impact on him was devastating. My heart broke for this pastor. But despite my compassion for him, I was strangely encouraged by his story. I felt a connection to him and a confidence that God was still with him. And if God was still with him, wasn't He still with me?

As he finished his story, I asked him how this trauma had impacted his faith. He said, "As bad as it hurts, if it happened so I can tell you and other pastors the story, and they are encouraged to know they are not alone, then it was worth it." Talk about taking one for the team. And as strange as it sounds, he was right. I did feel better.

What is it about shared misery that makes misery easier? What is it about someone else's pain that makes us feel better about our own? As a result of all my meetings with trainers, coaches, sages, and other rent-a-friends, I left with mere platitudes. Yet with this man, I left with hope. It must have something to do with community. Life is better lived together—especially in our pain.

My guess is that you know what it's like to feel exhausted. You keep using phrases like *When things settle down*—but things never do. Or you make bold predictions: "This year I'm going to achieve work/home balance," but balance seems to be a lost cause. You've downloaded countless apps to prioritize. You've subscribed to clubs, trainers, and diet plans to make your life better, yet you still feel overwhelmed. Then you go to church or spend time with Jesus and find your mind drifting back to yourself. Could it be that with all of the focus on yourself you have lost yourself?

There are some things you can only do on your own. Accept Christ, be baptized, and live out your giftedness, to name a few. Most other things can be done in community.

I think I know what you're thinking: *I know I should spend more time with others and stop focusing on myself.* True. But take it from an introverted control freak—the tendency for me and countless others is to walk away from such encounters thinking, *That was pointless.* Maybe instead of just acknowledging we are better together we need to find ways to really *connect with each other better.*

This book is designed to help you do just that—to find ways to connect, to be together . . . better. The first section deals with our apprehensions and arguments about community and our need for other people. Then we'll dive into how being together can make us better with God, with our families, and even with our personal issues and hopes.

My prayer for you as we start this journey is that you not only begin to understand the value of community but also see the God-given necessity for it. Whether you're an introvert, an extrovert, a control freak, a free spirit, a people pleaser, a curmudgeon, or something else, I hope you'll read on. We all can learn how to do life together . . . better.

Section 1

Help! Everyone Drives Me Crazy

I don't need anyone

I was in fourth grade when I first fell in "like."

I say *like* because *love* is a strong word. At the time, I still loved pizza as much as anything, so let's say I was in fourth grade when a girl finally didn't have cooties.

I'll call her Amanda to protect her identity. Thanks to the help of a mutual friend, I discovered that she reciprocated my feelings. So one hot Kansas day on the dusty playground in between the jungle gym and the monkey bars, we expressed our "like" for each other. Nothing they'd make a movie about—just "I like you." "I like you too." But in my mind, this was as good as when Han Solo told Princess Leia he loved her. (At least I didn't just hear "I know" as a response.)

This "like" of each other lasted all through fourth and fifth grades, but when sixth grade came around I began to sense she had lost that loving feeling. One day on the playground I approached her and asked her bluntly with fingers crossed, "Do you still like me?" Before she could reply, the bell rang. I had to wait four hours to get the answer at the bus stop. What would she say? How would I cope? Was there something I could say that might change her mind? *Help me, Lionel Richie.*

I walked out to the bus stop and waited for her class to come out. There she was. The smile had left her eyes. She looked at me and told me the words I was dreading: "Just as a friend." Our love story was over.

I walked to the bus trying to hold back the tears, but by the time I sat down I'm afraid the ugly cry had begun. My friend Scott was already in our bus seat. He looked at me, and he didn't even need to ask. He knew. He knew that Amanda had broken the heart of his best friend. And it was his duty to respond.

He stood up on his seat and used all his strength to open up that stubborn bus window that usually required a technician to move. He caught Amanda's eye as she marched to her bus like a tiger after a kill. He did what any loyal best friend would do—he began to shout profanities at her. Thank you, Scott, for saying what I wanted to but didn't out of my fear of going to hell.

I was not surprised that Scott had my back, because he had been my best friend for as long as I could remember. Scott's family lived three doors down from ours, and we spent our summers, weekends, and evenings after homework was done playing outside. I was Batman, he was Robin. I was Luke, he was Han. We played baseball, basketball, and football together. We rode our bikes all over town with quarters in our shoes to buy donuts and Big Gulps at the 7-Eleven. Scott and I were inseparable. And when Scott saw me take a light saber to the heart, he reacted the only way a best friend would. He avenged me.

I don't remember much after that moment. I probably had a panic attack. But if I know Scott, we probably played catch in the backyard for a few hours until I forgot all about the breakup.

There was something special about an elementary-age friend. It was friendship without the etiquette book. We never thought about niceties or appearances or dressing appropriately. We were just who we were. Sometimes weird. Often smelly. But always ourselves.

It's been over thirty years since that day, and I find friendship like that hard to come by. Why is loyalty like that so hard to find the older we get? Something happens after elementary school. We all grow up and worry about what others think of us. I think it has something to do with puberty. Suddenly we get concerned about wearing deodorant, battling acne, matching our clothes, and getting a date. And when you're trying to win the affection of someone, all friendships are negotiable.

Add social media and things get even more confusing. Think about the questions we wrestle with: If I have 1,500 friends, why am I so lonely? How come when I post something I only get a few "likes"? Why has everyone else been tagged in the picture, but not me? The struggle is real.

Is Together Really Better?

While we may smirk at the wounds from social media, we all have our friendship scars. It might have been a breakup. It could have been harsh words on the phone and then a hang-up. Or a string of painful words or deafening silence. It might have been betrayal or abandonment. However they come, we all have scars. And we remember the pain. We begin to wonder, *Is together really better?*

When my wife and I moved to California, we felt like fish out of water. We were desperate to find friendships and meaningful connections. We had moved two thousand miles away from our family and friends. Lorrie was home all day with our one-year-old daughter, and I was trying to lead a three-year-old church still meeting in a movie theater. The only people we knew were other church staff members.

So the first thing we did was join one of our church's small groups that happened to meet in our neighborhood. We were delighted to meet some new friends, and one couple in particular. They lived right around the corner from us, and even though their kids were older than ours, we had a lot in common. Our wives liked to walk and talk, and we (the other husband and I) enjoyed football and teasing each other when our teams lost. Their family was active in the church and seemed committed to the cause, so Lorrie and I felt blessed to be in relationship with them.

But after a few months I noticed things were changing. The familiar faces became more disgruntled. It started with occasional questions about the direction of the church and morphed into some venting about more depth. They were friends. I trusted them. And since I was a young leader, I let them help steer the ship. We added staff to teach classes they would enjoy. I made changes to my messages to meet their needs, but the comments continued.

Finally one day he took me to lunch and told me they were "moving on." His reason? They didn't like my teaching. *Wow! Tell me how you really feel.* They assured us we'd still be friends and get together, but you know how that goes. We didn't see them on Sundays or Mondays anymore. We stopped dropping by, and the friendship never recovered. It was hurtful for both Lorrie and me.

I remembered a time in second grade when a friend moved away from my class. I was very sad about this, so my mom offered this age-old proverb: "Make new friends, but keep the old, some are silver and the others gold." That sounded nice at the time, but now that I'm an adult it seems ridiculous. Friends that leave me are neither silver nor gold. They are more like dirt.

I wish that were the only time we experienced pain with friendships, but it's not. My guess is you have your own friendship wounds. You also know the pain of getting close to someone only to discover the feeling is not mutual and they walk away. No matter what reasons they give, and no matter how justifiable their actions, it still hurts. And it leaves a mark.

Collect enough of these friendship wounds and you begin to think, *I don't need anyone.* After all, why do I even need friends? This is especially true if you are married, with kids. Your life is busy enough. So you begin to think, *The people in my house are my friends. I don't have the time or emotional bandwidth for anyone else.* What we really mean is we don't want to risk being hurt again.

After a few decades of this you learn to put up some walls. Never let anyone see the real you. Only show them what they need to see. Keep everything on the surface. After all, didn't Solomon say, "Guard your heart"? Not needing anyone has its benefits.

Benefits of Going It Alone

I protect myself

The older you get the more relational lines you have to manage and thus the more opportunities to be hurt. When you're young, the only non-family relationships you manage are friends who live near you. When you get into junior high and high school, you have teammates, study groups, and social cliques to coordinate. Move on to college and you exchange your high school friends for dorm or fraternity friends.

After you graduate from college, things really start to get complicated. You have work friends, and if you get married, you have married friends. The odds of finding a couple you and your spouse *both* like are slim to nearly impossible. Then you have kids, and you develop friendships with the parents of your kids' friends.

The more relational lines you have to manage, the more opportunities you have to be hurt, the more wounds you receive, and the less trusting you become. How many people can you really trust, anyway? Who are all these people? If you share your heart with them, they may be gone tomorrow—or worse—they may share your heart with everyone they know. I heard someone say, "I find that if I just keep asking questions, I can listen or not, but I won't have to share anything about myself."

My wife and I went to dinner recently with a couple we would consider very close friends. We've been around each other for years. Our kids are Best Friends Forever (BFF) with their kids. We've traveled together, vacationed together, and shared lots of experiences. But as close as we are, I still found myself wondering at dinner what they were thinking of me. *Why didn't they laugh at that joke? Did I offend them? I wonder what they meant by that?*

Do you ever do that? *They didn't text right back—did I offend them?* After a while I feel like a criminal profiler trying to determine the suspect's motive. This only makes me want to deal less and less with people outside my immediate family. This only makes me want to deal less and less with people outside my immediate family.

So the walls go up. I keep it light. I protect myself from getting hurt. I walk fast and speak little. I say, "How're you doing?" and pray they don't answer me. It may be lonely, but it hurts less.

I get my way

Another perk of not needing anyone is I get to call the shots. I don't worry about your opinion. I don't stress about meeting your needs. I get to be in charge, and I get to take care of me.

Ever notice how your thoughts are consumed with *you*? You are the star of your own movie. So it only makes sense that everyone else should see themselves as supporting actors in your film, right? When your friends suggest a place to eat, your first thought is *Do I like that place?* And if you don't, you don't go. When neighbors invite us over, my only criteria is *Do I want to go?* Not *Would it be a good idea to get to know them better?* but rather *I just don't feel like it right now.*

I used to think having kids was the cure for all selfishness. After all, you are caring for a life, raising a child, providing for their every need. Surely after doing that for more than one child over several years, every ounce of selfishness would be gone. *Not so much.* For our six-year-old's birthday party she wanted to go to Chuck E. Cheese's with some friends. But in my mind, all I'm thinking is *I hate their pizza.* Not *But she'll love it.* Not *What a great idea for her and her friends* but *They have terrible food!* As much as she was excited about it, I found myself trying to figure out how I could talk her into going across the street to Chili's instead. I know Jesus said to deny yourself, take up your cross, and follow Him. But this is just dinner. Is it that big of a deal?

Why is it we can so easily become focused on ourselves even when our loved ones want something else? Here's why: Because at our core we are all selfish. We act like it's about self-preservation. We say we are just taking care of ourselves. We think somehow it's more spiritual to just need Jesus, not other people. But the truth is one person is easier to manage than many—especially when that one is me.

Even God Is in a Small Group

We don't know the exact audience for the book of Hebrews, but we know a few things about them. They were truly persecuted. They faced far worse than Chuck E. Cheese's pizza. Because they had become Christians, they faced the loss of businesses, homes, families, and even life itself. They knew people who had gone to prison for their faith. They knew fellow church members who had died because they refused to deny Christ.

After bearing witness to all of this, they had to be feeling a little bit of buyer's remorse. I'm sure they were building up relational walls and becoming suspicious of everyone. Who can I trust? Who will turn on me? Is it worth it? Everything about them could have closed the door and locked out the world. It's just my family and me. We'll get through this on our own.

That's why this letter is so powerful. The author knows they need this letter to help them keep the faith and not give up hope in Christ. He knows this letter will be read aloud in gatherings and passed from house to house. He knows he has a chance to capture their attention, direct them to the great God they now serve, and motivate them to stay the course.

So here's what he does—he paints beautiful word pictures to show God in all His fullness. He is more than a man named Jesus. He is more than a Spirit in the sky. And He is more than a Father to their fathers. He's all of the above. Before we conclude that we can live our lives alone, we need to realize something: God doesn't. God himself exists in community. Throughout this letter of encouragement and instruction, the author of Hebrews reminds his readers that although God doesn't *need* anyone, He exists in perfect community—a small group, if you will.

The Trinity has always been a difficult concept to explain, let alone understand. I've heard my share of metaphors to help us grasp it: water, steam, and ice . . . they're all H_2O. Or even sauce, pepperoni, and cheese . . . they all make up the same pizza. But these examples feel inadequate. After all, how do you describe the indescribable?

Though we serve only one God, and God is one, we know that God exists in three persons. The Father, the Son, and the Holy Spirit. We see all three present at creation. We hear God say, "Let us make man in *our* image" (Genesis 1:26 KJV). We see Jesus in the baptismal waters while His Father says, "Well done" and the Spirit descends like a dove. God exists in a small group. Perfect community.

Author Dale Bruner refers to God living in perfect community.[1] The Father is always pointing to the Son and the Spirit. The Son is always pointing to the Spirit and the Father. And the Spirit is always deferring to the Father and Son. They use phrases like *Look at Him, Worship Him, Be grateful He is coming.* They live in perfect submission to each other's glory. And yet they are all one. And though it's a little like trying to explain to a fish the concept of air, the author of Hebrews still wants his readers (including us) to be mindful of this relationship God lives in, even as complicated as it might seem.

> For God never said to any angel what he said to Jesus: "You are my Son. Today I have become your Father." God also said, "I will be his Father, and he will be my Son." And when he brought his supreme Son into the world, God said, "Let all of God's angels worship him."
>
> Hebrews 1:5–6

He points out the distinction of the Father and the Son and even the community of angels in heaven. Later on he gives further insight into the relationships between God the Father and God the Son.

> While Jesus was here on earth, he offered prayers and pleadings, with a loud cry and tears, to the one who could rescue him from death. And God heard his prayers because of his deep reverence for God. Even though Jesus was God's Son, he learned obedience from the things he suffered. In this way, God qualified him as a perfect High Priest, and he became the source of eternal salvation for all those who obey him.
>
> Hebrews 5:7–9

Here we see these two persons of the Trinity taking the label of Father and Son for the sake of all humanity. And then the Son becomes our High Priest by providing the sufficient sacrifice for our sin.

I recall talking with a seminary professor about the nature of the relationship of the Trinity. It was obvious I struck a nerve with him. He began to explain with precision and passion how the Father calls, the Son woos, and the Spirit guides us into relationship with God as a whole. By the end of his explanation there were tears running down his cheeks. The beauty of God existing in selfless community was overwhelming for him—and should be for all of us.

The idea that God created us because He was lonely is just not true. God was doing fine without us, in perfect harmony with himself in three persons. He didn't need us. He *wanted* us. He wanted us to experience what He experiences: perfect, yielding, submitting relationships.

So before we assume "I need no one" is a good core value to live by, we should consider this: Since we were created in God's image, we are created for community. Introverts and extroverts alike. We need others. We are truly better together. Maybe the question we need to wrestle with is: How do we do together better?

I miss the days when friendships were as easy as they were with Scott. My bet is you do too. We all need a Scott in our lives, and we all need to be a Scott to someone else. But to find that and be that, we must begin by admitting, "I actually *do* need someone." Yes, I'll get hurt, and they will too, but I'm more like God when I'm in community.

How to Be Together . . . Better

If we really are better together, perhaps what we need to learn is how to be together better. Here's the first step.

Admit I need others

I need more than just me. I actually need more than Jesus and me. Yes, Jesus is enough—for salvation. But to live, to thrive, to heal, and to know Jesus better, we need others. It is not good for us to be alone, so we must come to a place where, as much as we'd like to protect ourselves and get our way, we embrace the need for others in order to be our true selves.

Is it hard for you to admit that you truly *need* someone else? Is it difficult to push past the surface level of relationships and be vulnerable with another person? This is easier for some than for others. Extroverts and Influencers on personality tests find it simple to engage in conversation and easily confuse this for relational intimacy, but often it's hard for them to admit they need others. Introverts and Drivers find it hard to engage, but at least they know they lack social depth.[2] The difficulty for all of us is taking a willful step on our own to engage with those who may be even more hesitant than we are.

The first step is to admit "I need others." You don't have to fix all the issues around your selfish tendencies just yet. That will take time and the help of others. Before we go any further, though, we have to deal with a couple more roadblocks that will keep us from fully embracing community.

Discussion Questions

1. What did the author mean when he mentioned that God was "indescribable"? If that's the case, how do we come to know such a God?

2. How does knowing God make a difference in somebody's life?

3. How did you come to know God on a personal level? If you haven't come to know God, how do you see evidence that someone has?

4. Why do you believe that life is really better together, and what does that have to do with coming to know God?

5. Human beings are often selfish, self-centered, and self-serving. If this is often how we are naturally, why should we seek to become more humble and relational?

No one "gets" me

I hate camping. There, I said it. I love nature, I value fresh air, and I enjoy s'mores and hot dogs roasted over a campfire as much as the next guy. But it's the living outside that I don't get. I don't understand the fascination with working hard all year and then basically pretending to be homeless on vacation. Even if it is in the great outdoors.

But that being said, my love for my family eclipses my hatred for camping. So from time to time they exploit that love and talk me into going. Several years ago, when our girls were six and four, we were invited to join another family in our church to go camping. They love camping, they have a trailer, and they go often. In their minds, why wouldn't we enjoy it as much as they do?

I expressed some hesitation and claimed we didn't have a tent. They offered, "We have friends who will loan you an RV." My wife looked at me as if to say "You're out of excuses." She said, "Come on, the girls will love it." I reluctantly said, "Oh, all right—for the kids."

The day came for the journey and we made the hour-long drive to our destination.

During the unpacking, I was watching everyone else having a great time. Our kids were riding their bikes with their friends, my wife and the others were laughing while they unpacked. Me? I was feeling like a cross between Ebenezer Scrooge and Mr. Belvedere. It was clear to me that I was the only one who was miserable. No one else seemed to be viewing things the way I was.

Later we walked down to the beach and built sand castles. The kids were clearly having a ball. All I could think was *How many more hours?* I had brief moments of feeling hopeful, but then I remembered the sleeping conditions that awaited me. A bed filled with bugs and sand and chainsaw killers lurking in the campgrounds. At least that's what I pictured in my mind.

Apparently my distaste wasn't well concealed. Our friends joked about my "having a great time" while my wife gave me the "wife stare" that said "Act nice!" But as hard as I tried, I just couldn't. I was both miserable and confused. Why did no one else feel like I did? And why weren't they sympathetic to my misery?

After dinner and the s'mores, the kids headed for bed. We put them in the RV, tucked them in, and headed outside. We assured them we were just outside; if they needed anything we were close, everything was fine, so go to sleep. At least my wife believed everything was fine. I could still hear chainsaws.

We settled down by the fire with our friends. Conversation is easy around a campfire, I'll say that. I was actually beginning to relax a bit. Just about the time I was thinking this was better than terrible, I heard footsteps in the RV. The kids were up. To this day, I don't know what woke them, but in the dark, and in a strange place, they were having a hard time finding the door to get out. Before we could even get over to the RV, they began to bang on the side of the camper, yelling, "HELP! HELP! WE NEED HELP!"

It was horrifying, yet a bit funny. We finally got there and opened the door. They collapsed into our arms crying, and one of them yelled, "Why would you leave us alone!? Especially in times like these?" I wasn't sure what she meant by "times like these." Camping? The recession? Perhaps I'd mentioned the chainsaw . . . ?

My wife kept saying to them, "The door was unlocked." "No it wasn't!" they responded. "We couldn't find you. We didn't know how to get out! . . . Why weren't you here?" It didn't matter how much we tried to convince them that we were right outside and the door was unlocked. They were convinced they had been locked in.

I realized the girls weren't the only ones in a self-imposed prison that trip. I was too. I had convinced myself that because of my disdain for camping, I was unable to have fun. I locked myself into a belief that my comfort was the most important thing. Unfortunately, I'm able to do this even when I'm not camping. All of us are trapped in a self-imposed prison of isolation while we complain about being alone. But the door is locked from the inside.

Self-Imposed Prisons of Isolation

We don't intend to be alone. Even after our admission in the last chapter about our need for others, the truth is, we aren't sure if we *can* connect with others. After all, who will "get me"? And the older we get, the more we learn about ourselves, and the more we isolate ourselves.

It seems with every self-discovery comes greater alienation.

When we're young, we barely notice the difference between boys and girls. We just want to play and have fun. But as soon as we learn that girls have cooties or boys smell, we immediately cut our connection pool in half. Obviously, as we get older we find ways to re-engage with the other half, but we are always acutely aware of the differences.

High school taught us about socioeconomic differences. We all had our corner of the room in *The Breakfast Club*. Whether you were a jock, a prep, a geek, or a loner, everyone knew their place.

Then we go away to college and discover geographical differences. Many of us discover we have an accent. And our region of the country is known for a certain culture. If you're from the East, you might be characterized as elitist and aggressive. If you're from the Midwest, you might be thought of as a hick. If you are from the West Coast, everyone assumes you're a liberal and say *Dude* a lot. If you're from the South, they wonder if you took your sister to prom. And Texas . . . that's not even part of the South. Texas is just Texas.

In our twenties, we really begin to highlight our differences. That's when I learned the difference between introverts and extroverts. I discovered the reason why I always clashed with my roommates in college was because they were mostly extroverts and I wasn't. I also discovered why my wife and I are fine never leaving the house—we are both introverts.

Then I read a book telling me men are from Mars and women are from Venus. That brought great clarity as to why my wife and I thought differently—she was an alien. Later I learned about personality tests, StrengthsFinder, DISC assessments, and love languages.[1] I discovered I'm an intuitive, thinking, judgmental, cautious introvert who is strong in discipline, strategy, future focus, and responsibility, who appreciates words of affirmation. Needless to say, I've found very few people just like me!

So when I get my feelings hurt, when one person's conflict style opposes mine, when one person votes differently than I do, or when an extrovert demands I wave my hands in the air like I just don't care, it's easy for me to assume no one gets me.

Church Can Create Even More Segregation

While it seems we give some grace to those who are different from us personally and even politically, we often struggle to give grace to those who think differently theologically. It reminds me of the classic joke by Emo Philips I saw online.[2]

> Once I saw this guy on a bridge about to jump.
>
> I said, "Don't do it!"
>
> He said, "Nobody loves me."
>
> I said, "God loves you. Do you believe in God?"
>
> He said, "Yes."
>
> I said, "Are you a Christian or a Jew?"
>
> He said, "A Christian."
>
> I said, "Me, too! Protestant or Catholic?"
>
> He said, "Protestant."
>
> I said, "Me, too! What franchise?"
>
> He said, "Baptist."
>
> I said, "Me, too! Northern Baptist or Southern Baptist?"
>
> He said, "Northern Baptist."
>
> I said, "Me, too! Northern Conservative Baptist or Northern Liberal Baptist?"
>
> He said, "Northern Conservative Baptist."

I said, "Me, too! Northern Conservative Baptist Great Lakes Region or Northern Conservative Baptist Eastern Region?"

He said, "Northern Conservative Baptist Great Lakes Region."

I said, "Me, too! Northern Conservative Baptist Great Lakes Region Council of 1879 or Northern Conservative Baptist Great Lakes Region Council of 1912?"

He said, "Northern Conservative Baptist Great Lakes Region Council of 1912."

I said, "Die, heretic!" And I pushed him over.

My youngest daughter, Sidney, and I were out on our weekly daddy/daughter date. She was seven at the time, and when it came to our dates, she and I had several criteria. The place had to have ice cream, it had to have a playground, *and* it had to serve either coffee or Diet Coke (I have my standards). So when Sidney suggested McDonald's, I realized it met the criteria, so I agreed. I don't really have a problem with McDonald's. Partly because I, like 10 percent of the American workforce, was once employed by Ronald McDonald, but also because I enjoy a Big Mac as much as the next guy. So when she said McDonald's for our date, I didn't resist.

We walked beneath the golden arches and began to make our way to the counter. I was weighing the option of whether or not to super-size, when I noticed Sidney waving to someone at a table. It was a friend from her first-grade class at school. So we walked over to say hello, and I introduced myself to Sidney's friend's mother. We made small talk about how the girls knew each other and how great the school was, and then she hit me with this nugget of encouragement: "We've been to your church."

I've come to realize that statement can mean several things. It could mean we don't normally go to church, but we went to yours last Christmas or Easter. Or we've been, we liked it, and when we decide to go to church again, we'll go to yours.

So I said, "Oh, that's great. Thank you for coming. Love to have you again."

This is where she said something that caught me off guard.

"We're still trying to find the perfect church."

I wondered, *How could she not think that might be offensive?* I'm from the Midwest. We at least veil our insults with a hint of Southern charm. We would have said, "We've been awful busy and haven't been in a while" or just plain lied and said, "We loved it." How could she not think that she was basically saying to me, "We're looking for the perfect church, and yours isn't it"?

As she continued talking I could tell she had some church background. When people are fluent in phrases like *worship style* and *expository teaching* it's a dead giveaway. Apparently her husband preferred something more traditional while she enjoyed more "spirited" worship.

I ended the conversation with something like "Well, good luck with your search." Then I led Sidney away to the counter before I said anything I might regret. True to form for my personality, I spent the rest of the day (perhaps year) thinking about her comments.

My initial thoughts were rather shallow. They reflected my hurt feelings: *What's wrong with our church? Why did they not have a great experience? Was it the teaching?* (I convinced myself we must have had a guest preacher that day.)

But then my mind began to ponder the deeper issues going on. She was making her decision about where to go to church the same way my daughter and I had made our decision about where we'd go to lunch. While the requirements for church did not include ice cream, a playground, and Diet Coke, the basic question remained: Where can I find a place that meets *all* my needs?

45

Now, I'm not saying we go to that extreme, but most of us have our own religious preferences and styles, don't we? Are you Arminian or predestined to be a Calvinist? Are you Spirit-filled? Do you like John MacArthur? Do you think Joel Osteen is going to heaven? Do you enjoy traditional hymns or Passion remix? Is alcohol allowed? Or only at the wedding in Cana? Do you like secular music in church or just in the car on the way to church? Seems like even church can help create more isolation for us.

Attention, Church Shoppers

There's a common phrase I hear from Christians in our culture today: "I'm church shopping."

It happens when a family moves into a new town. They start looking online and visiting a different church every weekend. Sometimes I'll meet new families in our lobby and I'll ask how long they've been coming. They'll reply, "Oh, this is our first time. We are new to the area and are church shopping."

It also happens when something in their current church offends them. The music is too loud, the teaching struck a nerve, or someone they serve with has hurt their feelings. They begin to shop around, assuming "If I'm not happy here, I'll be happy somewhere else."

It even happens when a leader no longer feels needed. Perhaps the church has grown so fast or has made such significant changes in its leadership or direction that someone who's been there a long time suddenly feels disenfranchised or no longer needed. Larry Osborne states that when church staff or members feel they've lost power, prestige, or preference, they begin to get restless.[3] Then a couple of different things can begin to happen. At best, the person starts church shopping, looking for a better fit. At worst, they start blaming the church leadership and view the church as "no longer in God's will."

Church shopping can be the result of someone thinking *I've heard all this before.* Familiarity can breed contempt, and in our ever-changing culture, predictability can be the kiss of death. The moment a church member gets into a rut, or services get predictable, or even the teaching may seem to be subject matter they've already mastered, they assume it's time to look elsewhere. Combine that with a brand-new ministry across town that's buzzing with excitement, and the term *church shopping* is replaced by "God is doing something new over there, but not here." They conclude that God's Spirit has moved from their current church and into this new work, so it's time to move on. This can cause the most dedicated church people to go shopping for a better brand of church.

Studies show that church attendance is more sporadic than in years past. In previous generations, most churchgoers would say they attended two to three times a month; now the average is closer to once a month. Church loyalty is not what it once was, and when we decide to go, we figure our time is at a premium. We want to get the biggest bang for our buck, so we pick a place based on how many boxes are checked on our wish list.

- Entertaining, intellectually challenging, and emotionally soothing teaching
- Worship music that uses hymns and new songs, not too loud or too soft
- Good coffee (not just Folgers) and donuts (not just donut holes)
- Great kids' programs (that take place when my kids don't have sports)

- Women's studies (as long as they aren't going through a study I've already done)
- Men's fishing retreats
- A Singles Mingle group
- Vacation Bible school (to get my kids out of the house in the summer)
- All of the above

Now, I'm not saying preferences don't matter. And I'm not saying there aren't some deal breakers when it comes to the churches we choose to attend. But could it be that most of us, when we begin to shop for a church, are looking at the wrong list? After all, is perfection even an option?

The problem with all of these dividing issues is we are alienating ourselves in the one place that should be most unifying: church. With all of our groups, cliques, philosophies, strengths, styles, denominations, and preferences, no wonder we wake up one day and feel alone. No wonder we say, "No one gets me." In an effort to discover ourselves, we've lost our community. In an effort to specify our preferences, we've even lost our church.

The Cross Removes the Divisions

Paul writes that many of our divisions were removed through Jesus: "There is neither Jew nor Gentile, neither slave nor free, nor is there male and female, for you are all one in Christ Jesus" (Galatians 3:28 NIV). The beautiful imagery in this passage walks us through all the barriers in the Jewish temple. With each level there are new boundaries. No Gentiles past this point. No women past this point. Now only a priest may enter. When Jesus died, the heavy veil in the temple was torn in two and all the former boundaries were removed. I love that the veil was torn from the top to the bottom—as if to say, "This is from above and passed down to you." No more divisions. All are one in Jesus.

Paul will even take it further in his letter to the church in Colossae. Look at the groups he includes in this passage: "Here there is no Gentile or Jew, circumcised or uncircumcised, barbarian, Scythian, slave or free, but Christ is all, and is in all" (Colossians 3:11 NIV).

He even includes the barbarian and Scythian. These are truly "the least of these" since the term *barbarian* was another way of saying those who were "uncouth outsiders." And Scythians were the lowest form of barbarians, considered only a little better than wild beasts.

Paul says that in Christ, all these barriers come down.

If pious Jews and unclean Gentiles could learn to coexist, certainly introverts can put up with the shenanigans of extroverts. And if the refined Greeks could sit at a table with those just slightly better than wild beasts, then surely Baptists and Pentecostals can as well.

I love how author Max Lucado puts it:

A Brazilian Pentecostal taught me about prayer. A British Anglican by the name of C. S. Lewis put muscle in my faith. A Southern Baptist helped me understand grace. One Presbyterian, Steve Brown, taught me about God's sovereignty while another, Frederick Buechner, taught me about God's passion. A Catholic, Brennan Manning, convinced me that Jesus is relentlessly tender. I'm a better husband because I read James Dobson and a better preacher because I listened to Chuck Swindoll and Bill Hybels.[4]

Could it be that what makes us different can make us better?

Jesus Is Enough to Bring Us Together

Recently I led our congregation in an exercise I had experienced many years ago. I was teaching on Jesus' prayer for unity in John 17 and was trying to make the point that while Jesus prays for our unity, He does not demand us to be uniform. We are all different and come from different backgrounds. But through Jesus we can find common ground. So I took a moment to highlight some of the different backgrounds that bring us together. I listed denominations like Methodist, Pentecostal, Assemblies of God, Presbyterian, Episcopal, Baptist. I accentuated the difference between Protestant and Catholic. I even said that some may have no religious background. So on the count of three, I urged, "Let's all yell out our religious background." And we all heard a mishmash of words.

Then I said, on the count of three, let's all say the name of Jesus. "Jesus" was heard as clear as a bell. What unites us is what overlooks and overcomes all of our differences. We all need somebody. And when we find our common ground in Jesus, we can truly be better together.

Discussion Questions

1. What is your "self-imposed prison of isolation" that only you seem to find miserable in your life?

2. In what ways has the church often made these prisons worse in people's lives?

3. What do you think is the reason many well-meaning Christians often create so many obstacles when it comes to knowing God, when Jesus came to destroy these obstacles?

4. In what ways can we participate with God in bringing these obstacles down and unifying with one another?

3

Everyone else is an idiot

Our family was in a hurry and needed to get something to eat. So I did what any other responsible father would do. I took them to Wendy's drive-through. We love Wendy's. Everyone finds something they like, and they have a killer value menu. Plus my kids think the junior Frosty is the cutest thing they've ever seen. They have Diet Coke and chili, so I'm good.

We headed into the drive-through line. As we waited, I began asking for orders. My kids were about eight and six at the time so they still needed some coaching, but this time they had it down. Chicken nuggets, fries, junior Frosty. (Three of the four food groups.) My wife told me she wanted a salad, and I was ready for the chili. The order was locked and loaded when I pulled up to the speaker. "Welcome to Wendy's. May I take your order?" a young voice said. "Yes, I'd like two orders of chicken nuggets . . ." at which point I was interrupted.

"You said a chicken sandwich?" "No, two chicken nuggets." "Two chicken sandwiches?" I smiled at my family, trying to be patient. I thought I would mix it up to maybe help him out. "Let's go with two fries, a chicken salad, a chili, two junior Frostys, and two orders of chicken nuggets." "Would you like the combo meal with the chicken sandwiches?" he queried. "No," I said, "it's two chicken *nuggets*." "Oh, okay, chicken nuggets."

It was at this point that my six-year-old yelled out from the back seat loud enough for the speaker to pick it up: "Way to go, genius!" Oh my. My wife scolded her and I tried to support my wife, but the truth was, I was thinking the same thing as my daughter. I just wasn't going to say it! And if I were to say it, I'd wait till I rolled the window up and pulled forward.

This isn't my first drive-through. And I knew there were bigger issues than how the faux pas should have been handled. I was about to have to *see* this person. No escape was possible—the drive-through we were in was a lane barricaded by curbs and shrubs. I was going to look this person in the eye. I was praying he didn't go to my church. I approached the window with embarrassment, paid for and received my food, and drove away. Did I apologize? Did I even acknowledge it? No, I just played dumb. *Genius.*

As we drove and ate, my wife and I took turns instructing our kids on why we don't say those kinds of things—because Jesus wouldn't and because the food handlers could spit in your food. But when the kids went to bed, and my wife and I sat down for a quiet moment, we started laughing. We both have the spiritual gift of sarcasm, and it appears that gift might be genetic. It's likely our kids will face the battle we have faced our entire lives: When does funny become mean? As we laughed and talked we realized that our daughter simply said a version of what we were both thinking: *You're an idiot.*

I was in a drive-through by myself one time and all I needed was a cup of coffee. What made this even better was I had my own travel mug from that franchise. My only problem was that it had been sitting on my desk half full for about a month. I was nervous to look inside. Surely nothing too bad a little hot water wouldn't take care of. So as I got up to the window I said, "Will you please rinse this out with hot water before filling it?" "Of course, no problem," the barista assured me.

A few minutes later I got my coffee and was on my way. I was driving on the freeway when I decided to take my first drink. It was at this point that I discovered a couple of things. First, apparently when my barista said it was no problem to rinse out the cup . . . it was. Because it was clear he hadn't done it. Second, I discovered what happens in a cup that is half full and left on your desk for a month. It grows mold. So as I got a swallow of coffee I also got a lump of mold. What are your options as you are driving at sixty-five miles per hour bumper to bumper? Spitting was out of the question. But one thing was not in question: He was an idiot.

Sometimes I think, *Everyone is an idiot but me. Why can't you do things the way I would? Why didn't you think first? What does common sense tell you to do? If everyone would just do things the way I would, this world would be a much better place!* I'm sure I'm not the only one who feels this way. And if you don't, then you're either too holy, a liar, or an idiot.

Caution: Idiots Ahead

You're in line at the grocery store buying milk. That's it. So you get in the express line. But you are stuck behind someone who appears to be shopping for a boys' ranch. They clearly have more than fifteen items. *Idiot.*

You're driving down the highway around sixty-five miles an hour. And it's a sixty-five-mile-an-hour zone. But suddenly you hit the brakes because the car in front of you is going about forty and they have their turn signal on. Unless they are planning to take a right off a bridge, you assume they don't know it's on. Nor do they know the speed limit. When you finally get a chance to pass, you notice they are trying to text as they drive. *Idiot.*

Your cable television cuts out right during your favorite show. So you call customer service. Normally you try to avoid this, but this show matters to you. After pressing a variety of numbers upon instruction, you finally reach a human being who puts you on hold, transfers you, and then accidentally hangs up on you. *Idiot.*

These are all situations with people we don't even know. What about those we do?

What about when your neighbor decides to tune up his motorcycle at eleven o'clock at night as you are trying to get to bed in preparation for a busy day tomorrow?

What about when your aging parents decide to buy a motor home? You're not sure they should still be driving, let alone a house on wheels.

What about when you sit through hours and hours of meetings at work hearing one bad idea after another only to have someone table every initiative till next month? There's a day you'll never get back.

What about when your client who has been promising you a big contract suddenly pulls out at the end because it didn't "feel" right?

It's easy when you see all the ways things *could* have been handled differently, or the way *you* would have done things differently, to begin thinking, *Everyone is an idiot. No one brings any value to the table except me.* As a result, we start distrusting anyone else's input into our lives.

When we are left with questions about how to deal with our depression, handle our addiction, resolve our marriage tension, or help our kids with their anger, we wonder, *What good can anyone else do? I'll just figure this out on my own. After all, everyone else is an idiot.*

So how is being together really better? I may need people. And I may be able to find unity in Christ with others, but the question remains: Will they really add value?

One of the real obstacles in developing community with each other is when we view everyone as less than us and not worthy of our time.

Would Jesus Call Anyone an Idiot?

I know what you're thinking—He is God. He is perfect. But if anyone has the right to look down on others, it is the One who is above all. Think about all the opportunities He has to view everyone else as not worthy of His time. Scripture teaches that while He was on the earth, He was tempted in every way we are, and I think a big temptation He faced was to look at all His disciples and say, "You are idiots! Why am I wasting my time with you?"

Exhibit A

Jesus has just received the news that His cousin John the Baptist has been beheaded. Needing to process this grief, He withdrew for solitude, but the crowds wouldn't let Him rest. They pursued Him. "Where is He? Where's the miracle worker?" Think about the lack of emotional intelligence here from the crowds. They should have known to give Him some space. I would be tempted to let the crowds have it, if I were in Jesus' shoes: "Can't you see I need some alone time?"

But Jesus stops and takes care of the sick. In fact, Matthew tells us He had compassion on them! (See Matthew 14:14.) Even the disciples don't seem to protect Jesus. They not only let the crowds find Him, they come up and present problems and demands. "Hey, everyone's hungry, Jesus! And by everyone, I mean 5,000 people." (This number was probably closer to 15,000 since they typically only counted the men.) "You shouldn't let them go home hungry."

Jesus responds by challenging the disciples to do something to solve it. Their answer is to acquire a kid's sack lunch. Jesus makes something out of nothing. He prays and the disciples start passing out food till everyone is fed. They even have twelve baskets of leftovers.

As if this lack of faith from the disciples isn't enough to be labeled idiotic, not long after this they have a crowd of fewer people—just 4,000—and they are once again befuddled as to how they will be fed (Matthew 15). Jesus said to His disciples, "We need to feed them!" Their reply? "How? We only have seven loaves of bread and a few fish." Jesus didn't say (as I might have) "Seven loaves for 4,000? This is easier than five loaves for 5,000!" I'd be thinking *I've got to get some new disciples—some who can remember what happened a chapter ago.* Why would Jesus continue to hang around with these obviously deficient people?

Exhibit B

Later on in Jesus' ministry, we see another classic *duh* moment. Jesus has fed thousands from a "Happy Meal," He's cast out a demon from a young boy, and has even shown them Moses and Elijah at the transfiguration. And then He finds the disciples arguing about which one of them is the greatest.

Seriously? They are with Jesus! There's only one answer to that question. Much like we might discuss who the greatest quarterback of all time was or if LeBron James is better than Michael Jordan (Joe Montana, and no). Let's assume they are just contending for second place. Even then, it's a ridiculous discussion. There's Jesus . . . and then there's everyone else. No one even comes close.

But they think it might be one of them, so they are discussing it. This sounds similar to when James and John's mother came to Jesus asking if her boys could sit at the right and left of Him. *Really?* It's like their mom showing up at the first day of football tryouts and telling the coach they'd be starting, by the way. Jesus has got to be thinking, *I'm building my kingdom on these guys?*

As if that wasn't bad enough, it comes up again. This time it happens at the Passover meal before the crucifixion. We now refer to the Passover as the Last Supper (the scene where Jesus says, "Let's all get on one side of the table for a picture"). Jesus has just washed their feet. An act of service we will talk about till the end of time. And Luke tells us, "There was . . . a dispute among [the disciples] as to which of them should be considered the greatest" (Luke 22:24 NKJV). This sounds like a homeowners association meeting going badly. Jesus must be thinking, *I'm leaving my mission to these guys?*

Exhibit C

Peter is the brash, outspoken fisherman who can't keep his foot out of his mouth. You've got to love his courage and his ready-fire-aim mentality. Sometimes it serves him well—he's the first to confess Jesus as the Christ, the Messiah. But then right after that moment, Jesus states the fact that He will soon be killed, and Peter "took Him aside and began to rebuke Him" (Matthew 16:22 NKJV). How do you do that? How do you tell the Christ, the Messiah, He has it wrong and needs to get His facts straight? Jesus responds by saying, "Get behind me, Satan! You are a stumbling block to me" (v. 23 NIV).

Not long after, while experiencing the transfiguration and the presence of Moses and Elijah, Peter declares, in essence, "It's good we are here. Let me build a shelter for you, Moses, and Elijah." (See Matthew 17:4.) He's making plans for them to stay! While Jesus may be shaking His head at this, it's as if God the Father has had enough. The next verse reads: "While he was still speaking, behold, a bright cloud overshadowed them; and suddenly a voice came out of the cloud, saying, 'This is My beloved Son, in whom I am well pleased. Hear Him!'" (v. 5 NKJV).

I love that phrase *While [Peter] was still speaking* God interrupted him. In other words, "Peter, what you are saying is too stupid to continue. Let me step in and tell you what is really going on here."

But Peter's most epic collapse was declaring at the Last Supper, "I'll never leave you, Jesus. I'll follow you to the grave." Only to deny Him three times just hours later! Did Jesus ever think *Is this really the rock on which I'll build my church?*

While you and I might think these guys aren't worth our time, Jesus stayed in community with them. He saw no one as worthless, no one as less than, and no one as an idiot. He continued to trust, lead, and teach them. He gave them opportunities to represent Him. It was as if He enjoyed being with them. How could they have possibly been any benefit to Him? How could they have given Him anything other than heartburn or a few laughs?

Jesus Accepts Them as They Are

Even though Jesus was God in the flesh, the Christ, the Messiah, and held all the power and ability to show up, preach, teach, perform miracles, and declare "Follow me" all on His own, He still chose "we" over "me." He still valued community.

It started when He first called His disciples. He called Peter and his brother Andrew. Then James and his brother John. The latter two were nicknamed the Sons of Thunder. Someone may have had anger issues. He calls Simon, who is a political zealot, armed with more than a blog and social media account (a knife). He calls Bartholomew (aka Nathanael). This is the guy who basically called Jesus a redneck when he said, "Can anything good come out of Nazareth?" (See John 1:46.)

He also calls Matthew (aka Levi), who spent the better portion of his adult life cheating his fellow countrymen out of their hard-earned money by raising their taxes to line his pockets. And of course Judas Iscariot is also part of this motley crew.

Jesus surrounds himself with people we'd no doubt question like the Island of Misfit Toys. On our best days we'd query, "What were you thinking?" or "This seems a bit impulsive!" On our worst days? We would mutter, "Why pick these idiots?" Jesus could have done all He did alone, but He didn't. He said, "Follow Me, and I will make you become fishers of men" (Mark 1:17 NKJV).

Personally, I hesitate to bring others alongside me. I like to have people along who do what I say, but it's hard to have people walk with me who cause more trouble than they're worth. Much like with my kids, isn't it the hardest thing to watch them struggle with a project you know you could finish in half the time?

When my daughters were in elementary school, they would get frustrated with their math. "Dad, can you help me?" "Sure." You know how hard it is to not just fill in the blanks of the multiplication tables? It's easy, it's fun, it brings a sense of accomplishment, but we know the value is in their learning to do it for themselves, not just my doing it for them. Jesus teaches this to us. Though *I* could do it on my own, there is something to be said for *us* doing it together.

Jesus Empowers Them

This may be the biggest step in Jesus' leadership. He doesn't just accept His disciples, He empowers them to go out and act on His behalf. It's one thing to say "Follow me" and have them watch and learn. It's another to say "Go and do." In Mark 6, we read that Jesus called the disciples together and paired them up, then sent them out on His behalf.

> And he called the twelve and began to send them out two by two, and gave them authority over the unclean spirits. He charged them to take nothing for their journey except a staff—no bread, no bag, no money in their belts—but to wear sandals and not put on two tunics. And he said to them, "Whenever you enter a house, stay there until you depart from there. And if any place will not receive you and they will not listen to you, when you leave, shake off the dust that is on your feet as a testimony against them." So they went out and proclaimed that people should repent. And they cast out many demons and anointed with oil many who were sick and healed them.
>
> Mark 6:7–13 ESV

Think of the trust Jesus placed in them to represent Him, to heal with His power, and to cast out demons in His name. Sometimes it worked, and sometimes it didn't. On one occasion, we read that His disciples are unable to cast out a demon and they have to call for backup—Jesus. A man has come to them on behalf of his son, who is possessed by an evil spirit. He's asked the disciples to cast it out, but they are unable to. Jesus responds with a statement as close to "Everyone's an idiot" as we will hear from Him: "Jesus said to them, 'You faithless people! How long must I be with you? How long must I put up with you?'" (Mark 9:19). At first we think this is directed to the man with the possessed child, but it's actually directed to the disciples. "How long will we do this dance? How long will you lack faith?" But as frustrated as Jesus gets with them, He still maintains the relationship. Community is not lost.

> Afterward, when Jesus was alone in the house with his disciples, they asked him, "Why couldn't we cast out that evil spirit?" Jesus replied, "This kind can be cast out only by prayer."
>
> Mark 9:28–29

It's no wonder the disciples will ask Him soon after this, "Lord, teach us to pray" (Luke 11:1).

Despite their ineptitude, despite their idiot-like tendencies, Jesus still values this community. Why is that? Jesus knew what we have to learn: Not only do we need others, but they are not always exactly like us. They sometimes make mistakes. The value of community is found in being together, not in being the same.

Though Jesus was fully God, He was also fully human. As He walked this earth He experienced all the emotions we do, and in His darkest hours, He craved community.

It is at that Last Supper, the night before the crucifixion, He claims, "I've looked forward to this time together." (See Luke 22:15.) And then after the meal, they head out to the Mount of Olives, to the garden of Gethsemane, where He will pray. He asks them to come with Him and pray with Him. These are the same guys who didn't know how to pray. These are the same men who couldn't cast out a demon because they hadn't prayed. Yet Jesus says, "Stay with me and pray with me." When they fall asleep, you can feel His disappointment. "Couldn't you stay awake . . . for me?" (See Matthew 26:40.)

I've been to this spot outside Jerusalem. It's eerie to see that from the place where Jesus prayed He would have been able to see the Roman soldiers assemble and begin their torch-lit march to find Him in the garden. It is during this time He wants His friends with Him, even if they aren't the sharpest tools in the shed.

Hours later, Jesus has undergone the torture and trials of the crucifixion, and as He hangs on the cross He looks down and sees the lone friend left—John, standing next to His mother. And He says to him, "Please take care of my mom."

It shouldn't be surprising to us that Jesus would want to live with community. He himself is the second person in the Trinity and lives in constant community with God the Father and God the Spirit. The surprising thing is that Jesus puts up with subpar community. I mean, the Father and the Spirit are big shoes to fill.

But maybe this teaches us something about the servant mentality of Jesus. He's willing to satisfy His need for community with those who are not worthy of His company. He's willing to empower those who are not worthy of His power, and He's willing to share His deepest, darkest times with those who will fall asleep on Him during His greatest trial.

If Jesus finds life and mission are better together, shouldn't we?

Sometimes I'm the Idiot

If you're like me, you know the difficulty people can pose. They have different ideas from ours. Different personalities. Different agendas. And sometimes they don't do things the same way we would. But they are still created in the image of God and are worthy of community. Once we decide we need others and that Christ is the One who unifies us, we need to accept others with the same kind of grace Jesus extends to us.

The reality is that for as many times as I've been irritated in the drive-through, or upset at a coffeehouse, or annoyed at a red light, I've been that guy too. I've made people wait. I've made people angry. I've been the cause of someone else's frustration.

I've been the guy honking at a pedestrian. I've been the guy making fun of someone backstage with my mic still on. I've failed to bring my trash cans in on time. I've sent the wrong email to someone. I've failed to let someone know I'm running late. I've fallen asleep in a meeting. I've called someone the wrong name and acted like it was their fault. I've hurt my wife's feelings. I've been the guy yelling "Hurry up!" at my three-year-old in the parking lot.

Apparently while I was so busy claiming everyone *else* is an idiot, I forgot that I'm an idiot as well.

Learning how to do together better can be as simple as remembering I'm an idiot sometimes too.

Over the next few chapters we'll explore the many benefits that community can bring to our lives. It can actually help us connect with God, overcome our issues, and find a new depth to our relationships.

Discussion Questions

1. One of the core beliefs of the Christian faith is that Jesus was fully human and fully God. However, we often overlook that first part. Based on what you've read in this chapter, what is so significant about Jesus sharing our humanity?

2. How does Jesus being a human being inform us more about who God is and what God is like?

3. How does Jesus being a human being inform us more about who we are and who we would be if Jesus never existed?

4. Why is it important that Jesus doesn't simply accept us despite our idiocy, but also empowers us to move and act on His behalf in the world?

5. Why do you think Jesus chose to live in community, even with people who seemed to be slow to recognize who He was?

Section 2

Better Together . . . to Connect with God

Intimacy with God is deeper together

I'm an introvert. And like many introverts, I gain energy from being alone and feel drained after being with people for a long period of time. I like people, but I like being alone too. I like my family, but sitting alone watching sports after they've gone to bed is energizing for me.

There are times I schedule a lunch with someone and I go to the restaurant only to find they forgot our appointment. I'm sitting at a table by myself and I get the text: "Sorry, can we reschedule?" Traffic, meeting, forgot, doesn't matter. The server is usually very sympathetic. "Oh, I'm sorry you got stood up." "Oh, that's okay," I politely respond, but in my mind I'm thinking, *This is awesome.*

I'm even the weird type that can actually go to the movies alone. Not only do I not have to share the popcorn, there's no pressure to answer questions. There are no distractions. It's just me and the movie. I don't feel sad; I don't have a pity party. I don't feel like a loser. I'm a proud introvert.

Because of that, there are many practices of connecting with God that really suit me. There are the ancient practices of solitude and silence. This is taking time away to be alone. The purpose is to shut out the distractions and the noise that drown out His voice. I love solitude. I can drive for hours and just listen for God. I like to head out to the beach and sit there just to realize the presence of God.

Solitude and silence come naturally for the introvert.

There is the discipline of reading and prayer. Through reading books from desert fathers to current authors, I can sharpen my thinking and soothe my soul. Even if prayer doesn't come naturally for me, I can quietly talk to God in my mind rather easily due to my introversion.

I have found that introverts can even make public worship events solo experiences. For instance, it's not hard for an introvert to go to a church of thousands and still be alone. I can go by myself, sit by myself, and talk to no one except when I have to shake three hands during the greeting time. Singing alone, eyes closed, no distractions . . . then listening to the message focused on nothing but how this might apply to me . . . is wonderful.

But when I finish these things and come home, my tendency is to think, *Now I'm leaving my time with God. Back to the real world. I'll meet you another time, God.* As if I can only commune with God when I'm not with other people.

I like to think that Jesus was an introvert. Consider the facts:

Jesus once spent forty days in prayer. Alone. In the desert. While I consider myself a proud introvert, this is taking it to another level.

Mark tells us that Jesus once got up while it was still dark to be alone with His Father (Mark 1:35). It's been my observation that most people who are early risers are either farmers or in-troverts. Or introverted farmers. And when the disciples find Jesus and tell Him the crowds are looking for Him, He says, "Let's go somewhere else." Classic introversion.

Another time we read about Him out on a boat with His disciples. While they are tending to the sails, telling stories, and laughing at Peter's antics, Jesus quietly descends into the belly of the vessel to take a nap. Only introverts can nap when there's a party going on upstairs.

Even if you're not an introvert, I'll bet you can sympathize. You may feel like you are the only one in your home who is a Christian, so your faith is a "personal thing." You may be the only one at the office who knows the Lord, so your faith is either in secret, or you feel like a martyr. You stand out, but you stand alone. Or maybe Christians surround you, but you are the only one interested in actually growing in your faith. People are put off by your commitment to prayer and devotional time, so you begin to think, *I guess it's just me and Jesus.* When this has gone on for a while, there's a part of us that thinks that being a lone ranger may not only be the best way to deepen our faith, it may be the only way.

Despite how solo we may feel faith is at times, and despite how it can even be our preference, God reminds us that He can still be found among the masses. After all, though Jesus retreated, He always returned to the people.

After forty days in the desert, He returns—rested, renewed, and resolute. He gathers His disciples and they head to a wedding. Not a retreat, not a prayer vigil, but a crowded, festive wedding that gets so crazy they run out of wine. Jesus steps in and saves the day.

As for His early morning quiet time and quick escape from town, He then moves to another town, where He begins to preach to the crowds, telling them the kingdom of God is near.

Even though He takes a nap during a storm, after He's awakened by His frantic disciples, He goes upstairs to calm the storm and teach them a valuable lesson.

In fact, even at Jesus' darkest moment in life, hanging on the cross, He engaged with others. He took time to grant the dying request of a thief next to Him and made arrangements for the care of His mother with John, who stood below. Even if He was an introvert, He knew life and faith call us to live in community.

The Scriptures expand on this concept with instructions about our need for community. In fact, the author of Hebrews uses many *Let us* phrases. The receiving congregation is reminded there are some levels of faith that are best reached together rather than alone.

Faith Works Better in Community

The letter to the Hebrews begins with a reminder of the community's original confession of faith. As the writer lists the qualities of Christ and the tenets of their faith, he is declaring, "This is what we signed up for. This is the One we believe in." So it makes sense throughout the rest of the letter that he continues to exhort the believers to join together in their faith. Faith is more like basketball and less like golf. We need and rely on each other, and we get to our spiritual goals quicker together: "So **let us** come boldly to the throne of our gracious God. There we will receive his mercy, and we will find grace to help us when we need it most" (Hebrews 4:16, emphasis added). Granted, the real emphasis here is on where we receive mercy. It's found at the throne of God. But being together at His throne enables us to fully receive it when we "need it most."

I can't help but think about the men who brought their friend to Jesus on a mat. He'd been paralyzed for years. No doctor could help. He couldn't find a job. All he could do was sit on his mat on the city streets and ask for money. I can only imagine what his cardboard sign might say today: "Unable to work." "Been like this for life." "Please, have mercy."

The one bright spot? He had some friends. They were probably the ones who took him to the corner every morning and brought him home at night. When they heard the miracle worker was coming to town, they were the ones who decided to take him to Jesus.

The house was packed with people. There was no way in, but they were persistent. I can almost hear them saying, "We just have to get him in there—even if we have to tear the roof off." "Hey, not a bad idea!" So they climbed up to the roof, hoisted their friend up, and began to disassemble the shingles.

I've always wondered how willing the paralytic was. He had to have felt rather foolish being pulled up the side of the building. But after years of begging, pride was probably not something he struggled with.

Eventually they get the roof open and lower their friend down into the presence of Jesus. Jesus takes one look at them and offers mercy. He forgives the beggar of his sins and heals him of his paralysis. We don't know if this man had any faith when he went in, but he certainly had it when he left.

Could he have found forgiveness of sins through prayer alone in his closet? Sure. But he would have missed out on the healing. This small community of friends said, "Let's go to Jesus." And they found mercy and grace at a level they would not have found on their own.

In chapter 12 of Hebrews the author goes on to say, "Since we are receiving a Kingdom that is unshakable, *let us* be thankful and please God by worshiping him with holy fear and awe" (Hebrews 12:28, emphasis added). There is something we receive in corporate worship that we can't get on our own. We see other people worship. We hear other people's stories. And we see other people connect with God, even when we feel we aren't connecting.

This word *worship* (*latreuo*) can also be translated *service*. When we are thankful together . . . and when we please God together . . . we not only worship Him, but we are in a sense serving Him. As we serve each other, we serve our Lord.

Jesus tells us in the Sermon on the Mount that our service actually directs people to God: "In the same way, let your good deeds shine out for all to see, so that everyone will praise your heavenly Father" (Matthew 5:16).

One Sunday, after our 8:30 morning service was over, one of our ushers was going through the aisles picking up trash, preparing for the 10:00 service, when he found a wallet. He immediately took the wallet down to the guest services counter and said, "I found this wallet and wanted to turn it in just in case someone comes looking for it." The person behind the counter said, "Can I get your name in case they want to say thank-you or maybe even give you a reward?" The usher said, "No need . . . just praying it helps point someone to Jesus."

After the 11:30 service, someone came to the counter and said, "Is there a lost-and-found somewhere?" The attendant said, "This is it. What can I help you find?" He said, "I lost a wallet and I'm wondering if someone turned it in." After a few questions, the guest services volunteer handed the wallet over. The man did what most of us would do. He immediately checked to see if all the cash was still in it. He was shocked to see that it was. Then he said, "I had just cashed a check and had a couple hundred dollars in here. I can't believe it is still here. Maybe this church is all right."

Not long after that we learned more about his story. He was not a Christian and had started coming just to see what church was all about. This simple act that demonstrated integrity was enough to keep him coming back, and he was baptized the next Easter. In this case, his faith was a result of the witness of the community.

If you think about it, God's call on our lives is to love Him and love others. And that's impossible to do all by ourselves. We show our love by service. When I force myself out of my comfort zone to serve others, I find that I not only strengthen their faith, I deepen mine. I'm more like Jesus when I'm with others.

Jesus was the lead servant. He washed His disciples' feet, healed the sick, encouraged the broken, and even challenged the comfortable. All His actions were acts of service toward others. The only person I serve when I'm alone is me. When I'm alone, the world revolves around me. I get my way 100 percent of the time. I'm in complete control. Sometimes in that setting, I can even assume God is there to serve my bidding. But when I'm around others, I'm forced to yield to what others want. I don't always get my way. I have opportunities to meet needs, to serve someone besides myself.

We are never more like Jesus than when we serve.

This idea of service is not just seen by the church world. Even management expert Ichak Adizes reveals our need to live in service:

> Everything has a purpose, and that is to serve others. The lamp is here to shine light so I can type. The food I just ate is to nourish me. The bed across the room is for me to rest and sleep upon. Nothing in life exists for itself. Anything that serves only itself is like a cancer which serves no function but death. Some

people are cancerous. Existing for no one but themselves, they are exclusive takers. They take more from the land, water, and people than they leave behind. They destroy social value. They are socially cancerous.[1]

With service being such a valued character trait it should not surprise us that the writer of Hebrews instructs his readers not to give up connecting with God together: "And *let us* not neglect our meeting together, as some people do, but encourage one another, especially now that the day of his return is drawing near" (Hebrews 10:25, emphasis added).

We live in a culture where the average church attendance has dropped to one out of every three Sundays. It doesn't sound too bad to say, "I go to church every three weeks." But it sounds different to say, "Last year, I went to church a total of seventeen times." And if the weekend attendance is that low, the extra gatherings of small groups, mission trips, service projects, and Bible studies are even lower.

The author of Hebrews saw this coming and warned us: Don't give up meeting together. Our faith grows better together.

Faith Is Fulfilled in Community

The call for us to work as a team is not only because our faith works better but also because we are designed to find our deepest fulfillment this way. We were created in the image of God, and God exists in community. The Father, the Son, and the Holy Spirit live in perfect union of service acquiescing to each other's ability and glory.

Hebrews 1 refers back to Genesis 1. *Laleo* (Hebrews 1:1) seems to correlate with *amar* (Genesis 1:3, 6, 9, 11, 14, 20, 22, 24, 26, 28–29), highlighting God's act of "speaking" creation into being. This reminds us that God is still at work creating our world.

Some of us think that the apex of our faith experience comes by being awakened by a dream, a personal retreat, or even a silent epiphany while listening to a podcast, but the author of Hebrews would disagree. He encourages God's children to find even greater fulfillment by journeying in faith with each other.

I've found this to be true in my own life. Even though I logged over eight years in Bible College and seminary, my greatest faith experiences during that time were with people, not in what I was studying. And over the twenty years I've been doing ministry, my closest moments to Christ have involved people I've served or people who have served me. Here's where we find our richest fulfillment. "So then, since we have a great High Priest who has entered heaven, Jesus the Son of God, *let us* hold firmly to what we believe" (Hebrews 4:14, emphasis added).

Another theme of Hebrews is Jesus as High Priest. The author uses this tribal language to describe the whole community, which performs priestly tasks (13:15–16). Again, this notion is of a community in action as it follows God. While the emphasis is on Christ as our great High Priest, don't overlook the importance of how we approach Him collectively. There are just some things we wouldn't learn if left to our own devices. I like what author and speaker Bob Goff says: "You know why God doesn't speak to me audibly? Because then I wouldn't listen to you!"[2]

Like many churches, our church is organized into small groups of people that meet together during the week in order to take Sunday's message to greater depths, digging into how to apply it in practical ways. While our Life Groups can meet on any day of the week, my family and I participate in one that meets on Sunday afternoon.

I'll admit this is not the best day of the week for me when it comes to my attentiveness. I've just preached three times and have one more to go that evening, so by Sunday afternoon I'm often nearly catatonic. That being said, this group has our closest friends and neighbors in it, and since we've been together so long, we would hate to bail. So I go and make the most of it. And quite often, I'm reminded why Life Groups matter so much.

Not long ago we gathered together as we normally do. The only couple on time was the couple hosting the meeting. The rest of us arrived fashionably late. (That's "on time" in Southern California.) We all put our food offerings on the counter— some chips, vegetables, fruit, and cookies. When the coffee pot signaled the brew cycle was complete, we were ready to start.

We took our usual places in the living room. After an ice breaker and some catching up, we began to discuss the sermon. (This is always a bit awkward for me, because I'm usually the one who gave it.) As they talked, part of me was thinking *I've heard this. I taught this!* The other part of me was thinking *I'm exhausted.* Did I mention I'm an introvert?

That week we were talking about the story of Jesus calming the storm. I was sitting there, a bit comatose, when someone asked a good question. "Did the disciples even believe Jesus could actually calm the storm?" Silence. This was a question none of us had considered. Even me. When you look at the text, the disciples simply ask, "Teacher, don't you care that we're going to drown?" (Mark 4:38).

This prompted a discussion that took me to places with my faith I'd not explored while I was preparing the sermon. How often do I assume that God won't do something . . . or worse, *can't* do something? How often do I cry out, "Don't you care?" This led us into a beautiful prayer time where we declared our trust in God's care for us. This wouldn't have happened without my Life Group. In this group of caring believers this kind of thing has happened more than once.

Brennan Manning writes,

> We are not alone on the Yellow Brick Road. Traffic is heavy. Fellow travelers are everywhere. It isn't just me and Jesus anymore. The road is dotted with the moral and the immoral, the beautiful and the grungy . . . and the Rabbi's word, of course, is to love each person along the way.[3]

How to Come Together . . . Better

Putting all of this togetherness into practice can seem overwhelming, especially for us introverts. How do we make something so personal like our faith more of a group effort? How do we overcome our fears of being hurt and all the insecurities that come with opening up to other people?

Move from consumer to community

First, recognize that individuality is still important. You need your daily time with God. You need your prayer days. You need your solitude and silence. Just recognize this is not the end goal.

Second, make efforts to turn worship services into conversations. Instead of showing up late, leaving early, and evaluating how good the message was or whether or not you thought the music was too loud, make a decision that you'll engage in conversation with other people. When you get there, talk to the people around you—"How are you?" "How was your week?" Then on the way out make an effort to talk to others again. "What did God say to you today?" "What was it about God that overwhelmed you today?" "How can I pray for you this week?" When you pick up your kids from the children's ministry, take time to thank the volunteers who served. Thank the greeters on the way out. Thank the people who helped you get donuts.

Third, judge your experiences at church services through someone else's eyes. The best way to do this is by bringing a guest with you. You never see your church the way you should till you bring a friend. I've noticed that my non-Christian friends never say, "The music's too loud" or "I wish they played more hymns." They judge things based on "How will this save my marriage?" or "How will this help my drug-addicted teen?" If you're serving on the weekend, ask what kind of experience the people you served had. Ask them something specific: "Do you have any questions?" "Will you come back?" "How can I pray for you during the week?"

Next, during the week, find ways to share the Bible with others. Rather than just reading it on your own, read it with your family. Read it aloud at the dinner table. Email or text verses to one another. Caution: This shouldn't be done to teach or condemn—"I read this verse about greed and thought about your new car. Enjoy"—but rather to encourage: "I read this verse and thought it might brighten your day."

Finally, one of the best ways to deepen your faith is to pray for someone else's faith. One of the most overused phrases in the Christian community is "I'll be praying for you." But you know what is seldom heard? Follow-up to that request: "How is your job situation? I've been praying about it." Or "I've been praying about your daughter moving to college. How is she doing?" This is a fantastic way for us to live in community because so much of this can be done on email.

Keep a prayer journal of other people's needs, and then follow up. I know many families who keep Christmas cards from friends throughout the year and then pray for one family over dinner. Praying for others keeps us from getting in the rut of

"Help me, bless me, protect me." It forces us to think beyond our own needs.

Years ago, when I was serving as a college-age pastor, I traveled with a group of high school students to a summer camp. I was speaking at the event, and the high school pastor thought it would be good for me to get to know the kids who would be in college the next year.

It was a great week of fun, games, activities, and lots of worship. At the end of the final night, we went to our separate youth groups and reflected on the evening. People shared stories of what the music or the message meant to them personally. As the conversation became rather myopic, the youth pastor took us in another direction. He reminded us that we are on this journey together. And our journey didn't begin that night at this church camp event. It began when God created the world, and it continues with us now. With this in mind, he encouraged us to take a moment and remember the things that we, the people of God, had experienced together.

You could see the puzzled look on the students' faces. What was he talking about? Then he began to clarify. "I remember when WE crossed the Red Sea." "I remember when WE were fed by manna." "I remember when WE heard that Jesus was the Messiah." Now we got it.

Soon everyone began to participate. What was once a group of self-consumed navel-gazing teens processing things only by their own experience became a concert of remembrance. "I remember when we were saved by the ark." "I remember when we found out Jesus was alive." "I remember when we saw 3,000 baptized at Pentecost."

Our history goes back further than our lives. God is writing a story bigger than our own and developing a faith bigger than just mine. And it truly is better together.

Discussion Questions

1. What is the easiest way that you connect to God? What is more challenging for you?

2. How does being in community enhance your faith as a follower of Jesus?

3. How does serving contribute to this?

4. Is this notion of connecting to God through community new to you? What do you find most convincing about it? What do you find most uncomfortable?

5. How does the "just me and Jesus" attitude actually diminish our faith?

Joy is found quicker together

When my wife and I were dating, I was trying to make a good impression. I'd write notes, compose poetry; I even tackled singing a time or two. Whatever it took to win her heart. Flowers were certainly a given. So randomly I'd show up with some assortment of flowers. I'd even have them sent to her. Every time they were met with a rather polite yet underwhelming thank-you. For some reason this didn't seem to WOW her. I thought flowers in a relationship were a must. After all, didn't Barbra Streisand and Neil Diamond tell us how important it was?

After we had dated a few months, I felt secure enough in our relationship to finally ask, "I can't help but notice that you don't seem too impressed when I bring you flowers. Do you not enjoy flowers?" She said, "Sure, it's just that the father of the last guy I dated owned a flower shop. So I got them all the time. I guess I'm a little burnt out on them."

Well, all righty then. Once I got over the overwhelming emotions of being compared to the last guy, I decided I needed to pursue what *did* bring her happiness. Dinner out? Not so much. Movies? Slept through them. Miniature golf? Not even close. Finally it hit me—sweets. I'd take her out for desserts. Sometimes I'd bring her a brownie, and every now and then I'd get the box of chocolates. It was clear the way to her heart was through her sweet tooth!

Eventually, I deduced that there was one sweet that stood above the rest, and that was the chocolate chip cookie. She actually used to work at the Great American Cookie Company in the mall and would rave about them. She loved the single cookie, the big eighteen-inch cookie cake for birthdays, and occasionally the Double Doozie. For those not well versed in the Great American Cookie Company nomenclature, the Double Doozie is two chocolate chip cookies with icing in between. This was my ticket to her heart. I assumed the progression would go six Double Doozies, three mix tapes, then one engagement ring. And I was right! We got married, and I owe it all to the Double Doozie!

I continued my random acts of Doozie as a way to keep the home fires burning, but years later I apparently overshot. I thought since she loved the Double Doozie, certainly the bigger the better. And since she loved the big eighteen-inch cookie, then two of them would be even better. I called up our local cookie store and asked for something they'd never heard of before—an eighteen-inch Double Doozie. That's right, *two* big cookies with icing in between. How sickening is that? But, I thought, this is going to make her so happy! Sure, it might take her a year to eat it, but what smiles it will bring. When I went to the store to pick it up, they were staring at me, wondering who it was that ordered such a thing. Was he toothless? Had he already scheduled a trip to the hospital for a diabetic coma? I smiled, waved, and gladly paid for it. I hauled it out to the car, excited to see the response when I brought it home.

I drove cautiously, not wanting to damage this work of art. When I arrived at the house, I carefully took it inside and set it up on the dining room table. "Honey, I have something for you!" I called through the house. Lorrie was excited to see the cookie box, and I waited with anticipation as she opened it. But I was not prepared for her reaction. "Oh, that's just too much." *What?*

"But you love the Double Doozie and the Big Cookie . . . this is the best of both worlds!" I pleaded. (When you have to talk someone into liking your gift, it's probably not a good gift.) "Yes, but it's just too much." Then as a way to salvage the exchange, she said, "But thank you" with the same tone as when she got flowers! Instead of joy, it only brought disgust. For the next few days I watched her tear off pieces of the cookie and scrape off the icing. Apparently there is such a thing as too much of a good thing.

How is it possible for there to be too much of a good thing? Why is it that what makes us happy one day may not another? Why is it that what brings me great pleasure at one season of my life may not at another? Here's an example: When I was a kid I loved my Star Wars action figures. I had dozens of them, complete with all the ships and bases. (I'll spare you all their names.) But when I came across them in the attic the other day, they brought great nostalgia, but I had no desire to set them all up in the living room and have a battle.

This may be explained simply by growing up, but what about our adult interests? Our garages, attics, basements, storage units, and that coveted space underneath the bed are often cluttered with once promising ideas. From Bowflexes to ab rollers, remote-control cars to drones, and scrapbooking supplies to decoupage ideas, we all have things that bring momentary happiness but soon fade.

Here's the difference: Happiness is an experience. Joy is a choice.

Happiness comes and goes. One day it comes from a cookie, another from flowers. And sometimes from Darth Vader. Why is it we find such happiness at Disneyland one trip, but the next time we go we don't have much fun? Happiness is an emotion. Some days you wake up happy. Some days you wake up cranky. You see this in your spouse. There are some days you are drawn to them because of their exuberance, and other times you decide to go outside and rotate the tires just to be alone. It reminds me of a sign I once saw: *I'm so miserable without you, it's like you are still here.* The point? Keeping happiness is like trying to catch the wind.

And we do our best to catch the wind. We spend much of our lives looking for joy through happiness. We wonder what will make us happy now. Not what used to . . . that doesn't work anymore . . . but what will satisfy us today?

Eugene Peterson once said: "The enormous entertainment industry in America is a sign of the depletion of joy in our culture. Society is a bored, gluttonous king employing a court jester to divert it after an overindulgent meal."[1]

Happiness I can find, and it can find me. But joy is something else. Call it fulfillment. Call it contentment. Real true deep-seated joy is not whimsical. It doesn't come and go. It's a result of something. It's a choice.

One of the first thoughts we have about joy is that it's a fruit of the Spirit. Paul tells us the result of being in Christ and the Holy Spirit living in us is that we will be known for our love, peace, patience, kindness, goodness, gentleness, faithfulness, self-control, and yes . . . our joy.

For much of my life I've viewed the fruit of the Spirit as a to-do list for me, something I needed to do on my own. Oh, sure, the Holy Spirit is there to assist, but I always viewed Him as more of a foreman—standing around making sure that I was working. "Hurry up and have more patience!" "Watch yourself . . . you need more self-control!" So, the idea of producing joy, or choosing joy, was up to me. On my own. Try harder.

Yet when you look at the entirety of Scripture, you realize that joy comes *from* the Holy Spirit. We don't work it up. And it's rarely something we experience internally. Especially in the Old Testament, you see that joy has a cause and an expression, sometimes in feasts and other times in festivals. It was both a choice and a celebration. Joy was to be enjoyed with others—not just by the Holy Spirit and me. It's as if joy is the result of our freedom found in God that can be expressed best as a group.

My pushback is "Why?" If joy is a choice and it's a result of my submission to the Holy Spirit, why do I need others to experience it? Maybe you've thought, *I've got this myself. I can find joy. I just need some downtime. A "me" party. Perhaps a day spa. Surely that will bring joy.* You will find *happiness* doing those things. You'll have an endorphin rush or a dopamine dump, and you'll even feel rested. But it's not lasting joy.

What if it's just you and the Holy Spirit? Sure. I won't limit what the Holy Spirit can do in your life. But it does seem that the Holy Spirit uses others around us to help us experience true joy. Joy is found quicker together.

Marching toward Joy Together

The ancient Hebrew people seemed to understand this. In our Old Testament Scriptures is a grouping of songs that were written by David, Solomon, and others (some believe Hezekiah and Isaiah). The book of Psalms is composed of 150 prayers and songs to God collected over a period of hundreds of years, particularly in the time of the Babylonian exile. Within these psalms are a group of songs called "A song of ascents" (Psalms 120–134). (*The New International Version* uses this as a title for each of these psalms.) They are named "A song of ascents" because they were sung as they ascended. There are different theories about where the name came from: (1) They were songs sung or recited by people returning to Jerusalem directly from the Babylonian exile; (2) They were called "A song of ascents" or "A song for pilgrims ascending to Jerusalem" (NLT) because their rhythm or tone scales upward as each of them progresses; (3) They were the songs sung by Hebrew pilgrims who went to worship at the temple in Jerusalem three times each year (for the Feast of Tabernacles, Passover, and Pentecost).

How ever they came to be called "A song of ascents," the meaning is clear: They marched toward joy and fulfillment *together*.

Look at how Isaiah describes this ascent:

> Many peoples shall come, and say: "Come, let us go up to the mountain of the LORD, to the house of the God of Jacob, that he may teach us his ways and that we may walk in his paths."
>
> 2:3 ESV

> You shall have a song as in the night when a holy feast is kept, and gladness of heart, as when one sets out to the sound of the flute to go to the mountain of the LORD, to the Rock of Israel.
>
> 30:29 ESV

This journey not only engages the community, it engages them *with God*. In doing this, joy is achieved.

This idea is not only in the Old Testament with the ancient Hebrews but also in the New Testament with the church. Being a follower of Jesus is not just being regarded as a disciple, but in Hebrews the author draws parallels to us as fellow pilgrims like Abraham. (See Hebrews 11:9–16.) The differences are distinct: As a disciple, or learner, we spend our lives learning from our master and appropriating that knowledge to skill. But as a pilgrim, we spend our lives traveling, sometimes without a particular destination other than the heart of God. And we do this together. This is exactly what the Hebrew people did as they marched toward Jerusalem three times a year.

On my trips to Jerusalem, the temple steps always humble me. It is here you can be 100 percent assured that Jesus walked these steps. And it is also the place where for centuries the Jewish people made their way up these stairs headed to the temple. Three times a year, they made their pilgrimage from wherever they lived to worship Yahweh. No matter where they were coming from, when they made it to Jerusalem, they would ascend. Partly because Jerusalem is built on a hill, but also because of these steps.

They would travel in groups; they would caravan with families, and they would do so remembering the faithfulness of God. They would recite these songs of David, these psalms from their ancestors, these calls to worship, and they would celebrate. In doing so, they achieved joy.

What are the choices we must make to achieve joy? Take a look at how they did this.

They chose to worship with others

"I rejoiced with those who said to me, 'Let us go to the house of the LORD.' Our feet are standing in your gates, Jerusalem" (Psalm 122:1–2 NIV).

They were thrilled to head to the temple. In our culture, church attendance is declining, but for them the very thought of the journey to Jerusalem with everyone else brought joy.

Think about how we distort this principle.

We choose to worship ALONE. I can go on a bike ride and listen to a sermon or a playlist of worship music, but have I really experienced church?

We choose to worship OURSELVES. We are consumed with our appearance, our health, our image, and how others see us. We take 100 selfies to find one we like. We stew over why people haven't liked our social media post.

We choose to worship OTHERS. We bend over backward to make someone else happy or to see their smile. Most notably our children. We worship at the altar of public opinion and approval.

The Jews got the order right. They worshiped God with others.

They chose to encourage each other

You can hear them admonish one another:

Pray for the peace of Jerusalem: "May those who love you be secure. May there be peace within your walls and security within your citadels." For the sake of my family and friends, I will say, "Peace be within you." For the sake of the house of the LORD our God, I will seek your prosperity.

Psalm 122:6–9 NIV

Do you hear the choices made in that? I choose to pray for you. I choose to find your success and prosperity. I pray for your peace. And in this I find joy.

This continues in the prayers of pleading.

Have mercy on us, LORD, have mercy on us, for we have endured no end of contempt. We have endured no end of ridicule from the arrogant, of contempt from the proud.

Psalm 123:3–4 NIV

No praying only for themselves. No pet projects only for their pleasure, but a communal, almost national type of prayer. And in doing so, they seemed to find great joy.

They chose to be grateful about fellowship

It continues in the prayers of gratitude.

If the LORD had not been on *our* side . . . they would have swallowed us alive . . . the flood would have engulfed us, the torrent would have swept over us, the raging waters would have swept us away. Praise be to the LORD who has not let *us* be torn by their teeth.

Psalm 124:1–6 NIV

Serving God is not a solo sport. This is not a list of things *I* am thankful for, but rather what *we* are grateful for. What God has done for our community. With every recitation, they chose joy: "The LORD has done great things for us, and we are filled with joy" (Psalm 126:3 NIV).

Eugene Peterson reminds us that joy is not a requirement of Christian discipleship but rather a consequence. When we choose faith and obedience, we find joy along the way. We choose joy when we choose to obey. Joy for the Hebrew people was found when they chose to march toward Jerusalem. Together.

"Blessed is every one who fears the LORD, who walks in His ways" (Psalm 128:1 NKJV).

This is the beginning of our joy. This joy finds its completion in being in the temple together:

Behold, how good and pleasant it is when brothers dwell in unity! It is like the precious oil on the head, running down on the beard, on the beard of Aaron, running down on the collar of his robes! It is like the dew of Hermon, which falls on the mountains of Zion! For there the LORD has commanded the blessing, life forevermore.

Psalm 133 ESV

Look at the rich imagery here. When we are together, when we are unified, and when we are at peace with one another, it is like the anointing of God has been poured out on us. While I often thought worship was best done alone, or my anointing from God came when I was away on a three-day fasting retreat, the psalmist says the opposite. It comes when we join together to worship as a community.

In mentioning the anointing of Aaron, the psalm is evoking memories of the scent of the oil that's uniquely prepared for the priesthood. No one is supposed to replicate that recipe for any other purpose. It is so distinct that all would know its aroma. This is the oil used for the anointing of priests in ancient Israel. By implication, we are part of the priesthood when we are together. This union is of the Lord.

David goes on to use the image of the dew of Mount Hermon. This mountain sits at 9,000 feet above sea level and has always been known for its lush greenery, even during the summer months. It is this type of blessing: like the dew falling on Mount Zion.

This All Begins with God

All of this is a result of God's decision to bless us. Where God's people are living together in unity, it is there the Lord commands His blessing. And this blessing brings life evermore.

Unity is an interesting concept. Jesus prays for it, and God is the only One who can give it: "Make every effort to keep the unity of the Spirit through the bond of peace" (Ephesians 4:3 NIV). It's not something we force. It's something we keep or embrace. Because of Jesus, all the things that once separated us—ethnicity, gender, heritage, even personality—can be overcome to enjoy unity. This unity brings joy, but it must be maintained.

Joy chosen. Joy received. Joy together.

See what God sees in others

Perhaps we could learn something from this Hebrew sojourn. We can choose to worship with others. We can choose to encourage one another during the week. We can choose to be grateful for what we have and the people we have in our lives. After all, these gifts are all from God. He's obviously not just crazy about *you*, but also the people we think are crazy.

When your schedule is overcrowded and your margin is slim, it's easy to get exhausted and frustrated with people. "Way to go, genius!" becomes my mantra. It's easy for me to think in these moments that the problem is not my schedule but the people in it. So the easy solution is to get away.

Remember the advertising slogan of a popular airline? Characters were shown in embarrassing or exhausting situations and covered by the line *"Wanna get away?"* We all want to get away. Maybe your mind drifts to an island setting where it's just you on the beach watching the sun go down. Or maybe your daydream is a quiet evening at home with no one around, just you and your favorite chair, a book, and a cup of tea. Maybe it's a long walk in the woods or a five-mile run. We all have our dream destination, but the one thing about most of our dreams is we are always *alone*. We think the way to find happiness, even joy, is to get away from all these crazy people. "Table for one, please."

Every few months I try to take some time away to pray, study, or write. I find myself craving these times. Longing for them. I put them on the calendar and count down the days. Every time I'm in the lobby at the church and someone says, "Pastor, that message reminded me of a better one I heard on TV this morning . . ." I think, *Twelve more days!* Yet, when the day comes, I'm always amazed how quickly I actually miss people.

A few years ago, I decided for my day away I'd rent a convertible and drive up the coast. We are only forty-five minutes from the beach. I knew the beach would be therapeutic. I had the convertible, my sunglasses, and James Taylor on the radio. Everything was set for a relaxing day of solitude. But I learned two things that day: First, sunscreen would have been a good idea. Second, after about an hour, I found myself thinking *This would be more fun with my family in the car to share it with me.*

About a year later I needed to get away to finish a book I was working on. A wonderful family in our church has a cabin in the mountains and offered it to us when needed. I booked two days up there and threw a duffel bag together with clothes, books, and my laptop and drove two hours up into the mountains.

I was excited about the alone time and getting some writing done. My head was spinning with ideas and phrases to put down as soon as I could. I pulled up to the cabin, unpacked, and set up my laptop, and in about an hour I found myself texting people back home. I texted my wife: *"Hey, how you doing?"* I texted people at the office: *"What's going on?"* I texted my kids: *"How was school today?"* I worked another hour and thought, *I wonder what's happening on Facebook.* I got a lot of work done, but I actually left earlier than anticipated and couldn't wait to get home. Why? I had happiness, but I was missing joy.

While processing this as I drove down the mountain I remembered a time I drove out to a monastery for some alone time. We were still living in Kentucky at the time, and Abbey of Gethsemani was about an hour away. This was the former home of the great sage Thomas Merton. I loved the drive and the silence and solitude that immediately fell on me as I drove up.

While I wandered the grounds, maintaining the vow of silence, I would read, write, pray, and wait. I'd wait for the tolling bells to signal the time to convene in the chapel for prayer. I looked forward to seeing some other faces. Even if we didn't speak more than just "Peace be with you," it was meaningful interaction. And apparently I wasn't the only one who felt that way. I watched as the monks made their way to embrace one another, smiling and greeting. There truly is happiness in being alone, but joy in being together.

Discussion Questions

1. What are some misconceptions of the church you often hear? Do you share them?

2. In your understanding, what is the role of the church in the world?

3. We sometimes think we can worship God better alone. If this is so, why do you think we continually feel the need to attend a church service?

Anxiety is calmed together

Growing up, I had the common fears: the monster in the closet, the man hiding behind the shower curtain, and of course the Howdy Doody doll.[1] Anyone else? That was my limit, until I made the mistake of watching the movie *Poltergeist*. Then suddenly clowns made the list. I always knew they were up to something, and this movie let me know they were lurking under my bed!

And yet, despite growing up watching movies about crazy clowns, vampires, and homicidal hockey-mask-wearing teens, I, like every friend I had, would say every Halloween, "Let's go through a haunted house!" It always seemed like a great idea when we were discussing it over bologna sandwiches in the safety of the lunchroom in the light of day. We were all tough twelve-year-olds just looking for a fear to conquer. Bring it on, leatherhead! You don't scare us, Michael Myers! (Just leave Howdy Doody and Bozo the clown out of this.)

One year we decided to follow through on our threats. How we talked our moms into letting us go, I'll never understand, but they dropped us off outside of the local haunted house. We gathered outside with the bravest of intentions, but now that it was dark, and we could hear the screams from within, and our mothers were long gone, we were suddenly a bit hesitant. One of us suggested they might not let us in due to our age and height. Another friend suddenly couldn't find his money. I think I tried to fake an injury. Whatever it would take to be able to walk away with a reasonable excuse and a shred of dignity.

But after some pep talks to each other, and some older kids telling us to hurry up and get in line, we began the "death" march with one resolve: We will stay together. I remember at one point locking arms. Someone might have led us in a chorus of "We will all go down together." But as the entrance drew closer, we began to argue: "I'm not going first!" Another said, "I'm not going last." "Let's lock arms back-to-back . . . we'll go through this as a circle." That sounded good to me.

The next seven minutes seemed like an eternity. When you experience the fight-or-flight syndrome together with arms locked, it can create quite a conundrum. Every time we'd hear a chainsaw fire up or someone would lunge out from behind a curtain, half of us would run and the other half would want to fight. I can neither confirm nor deny if any of us burst into tears or yelled "Mommy!" We bumped and tripped our way through the experience. Once it was over, we all celebrated with high fives and cheers, declaring, "That wasn't even scary!"

Years later, I found myself outside a haunted house with my daughters and their friends. Their elementary school was putting on a Halloween carnival and I thought, "Why not? After all, I survived, they will too." And sure enough, they huddled with their friends outside, fearing what might await them inside. Some got nervous and wanted to back out—or as we affectionately refer to it—"chicken out." But others tried to persuade them to stay. I was laughing at them, and at the memory of how much my group of preteen friends acted a lot like these preteen girls. Finally I gave them the secret: You have to do this together. Lock arms, circle up, and walk bravely into the darkness. They didn't buy it, so they bailed.

I've come to discover that life can sometimes feel like a long walk through a haunted house. We all live with certain fears, and they come in all shapes and sizes.

For some they look like scary monsters

We look at our fears and see the regrets of the past—the date we wish we'd never gone on, the bar we wish we'd never entered, or the job we wish we'd never taken. Their impact is still painful and ever present. These monsters leave shame and fear behind them. They cause us to stand still in our lives. They trick us into never trusting again. They convince us that no one else has ever gone through the same thing, and no one else would ever understand what we are feeling. So we keep the monster in the closet. The monster knows that if he stays hidden, he'll only grow.

For some they look like clowns

These are decisions that once appeared to be good but turned sinister—the business deal that would change everything, the marriage proposal that seemed too good to be true (and was), or the investment that promised a life of luxury but didn't come through. One of the biggest clowns we face is consumer debt. We are all allured by the shiny, the new, and the instant.

I remember the first time I filled out a credit card application. We were newlyweds standing in line at Target. I saw the

Discover Card form and thought, *That's something I should do now that I'm a married adult.* It seemed like a good idea at the time. After all, you need to establish credit to get credit. Right? We'd been living on cash up until that point, but this promised a new taste of freedom. No longer did I have to say *no.* "Let's go out to eat." "Can we afford it?" "Discover says we can." "Let's get that new computer." "Can we afford it?" "Discover says YES!"

This began an ongoing process of maxing out the card, then paying it off. Secretly I thought, *I must be the only one who struggles with this.* This is what many of us think who have been on the debt roller coaster.

For some it's standing outside a haunted house

There's a risk ahead of us and we just can't get up the nerve to step into it. It might be the commitment of marriage, or the sacrifice of having kids, or the unknown of a career change. We are paralyzed with fear to the point that we settle for lives on the sideline, living vicariously through other people. We scroll through social media, reading about others' lives and think, *That must be nice.* But we are too scared to take the risk.

Our problem is not the monster, the clown, or even the haunted house. Our problem is that we have failed to lock arms, circle up, and walk bravely into the darkness.

Rationalize or Catastrophize?

When it's just me, I drift toward one of two things: rationalize it or catastrophize it.

If my fear is my health or my finances, I'll likely keep that to myself and rationalize how it's really a good thing. Have you ever said, "The last time I worried about the lump on my neck it turned out to be nothing, so that's the way to approach it. Worry, stress? Look on WebMD and hope it goes away. It's science."

Or maybe you do this with your finances: "We give nothing, we save nothing, and we spend 125 percent of our income, but we'll eventually get it together. It will all work out. We play the lottery; hopefully we'll win big." Maybe you're even so bold as to secretly bank on someone in your family dying and leaving you something in their will. But be warned: When someone in your family knows their death will fund your retirement it tends to taint the holidays.

The other extreme is to catastrophize everything. Yes, I know it's a little used word, but it works for this analogy. Every fear is "the end of days." We lose an account and we immediately think we'll be pushing a shopping cart down the street. Your son doesn't text back immediately, so you assume he's dead in a ditch or has joined a gang. You call your spouse and get no answer, so you assume he or she is having an affair. It's amazing how much sense our nonsense can make when we're all alone in the courtroom of our mind.

The Value of Walking Together

Scripture shows us examples of ordinary people facing extraordinary fears simply by locking arms with others and walking bravely into the dark.

David had been freshly anointed by Samuel to be the next king. Consequently he's thrust into pressures no one in his family can understand. He's all alone with his concerns. His brothers were all passed over and have to be a bit annoyed by their "better than us" younger brother, so they offer no support.

He then has to wait till he takes the throne, so he spends his days serving his brothers, herding sheep, and oh, killing a giant. After that he's suddenly on the current king's radar (Saul). "Who is this kid, what's this nonsense about him becoming king, and why do the people like him more than me?" How would David deal with his legitimate fear of the mad king and the upcoming tenure of leadership?

He becomes close friends with the only other person who might understand the pressure he's under—Saul's son Jonathan. Even though Jonathan is not going to get the throne, he befriends David, the one who is. And their friendship gets them through some dark days of battle.

After David has to fight for his life, he takes his friendship skills and opens his heart to a group of warriors and renegades on the run. They become fast friends, often referred to as David's mighty men. These guys develop such a friendship with David that they would do anything for him. David has to hold them back from killing Saul when the opportunity arises, and one day David remarks how a drink from his "hometown well" would sure taste good . . . so his friends go and fill a canteen for him at great danger to themselves. David is so humbled by their heroism he can't even drink it. This friendship not only saved his life and met his basic needs but also helped him walk through the fear that came as he waited to be crowned king.

The moment David goes solo and isolates himself from everyone is when he makes his biggest mistakes. He wanders out on the roof to watch a woman bathe from a distance. Eventually he commits adultery with her and arranges to get her husband killed on the battlefield, and David's kingdom never recovers. The only way God gets his attention to face the monsters under his bed is by sending a prophet to speak truth to him. Once

David stopped locking arms, he wandered into the dark on his own . . . and the monsters were waiting.

Esther was a beautiful queen in waiting. She is one of many in a powerful pagan king's harem. She's basically a child bride, a slave, who's selected to become the new queen. How will she face her fears? She relies on a friendship with her relative Mordecai. He advises her how to navigate the tricky waters of this complicated marriage. And then, when she hears that her entire race may face genocide, her friendship with Mordecai helps her leverage her relationship with the king to face her fears and save her people from impending doom.

Mary, the mother of Jesus, found herself in a strange predicament: She was the chosen one to give birth to the Messiah. Talk about being in a unique situation! Even with our diverse personality types, StrengthsFinder assessments, DISC assessment test, and ethnic backgrounds, we've never known a narrowing of the playing field like this. If there was anyone who could have let anxiety turn them inward, if there was anyone who could have literally said, "It's just Jesus and me" . . . it was Mary. Even Joseph didn't completely understand. But Mary took solace in her friendship with her cousin Elizabeth. It's interesting to me that she had the biggest decision to process, and she had no one who would understand, but she still reached out and confided in another. She locked arms with her cousin and they marched into the dark together.

But Wait . . . I've Tried That

That being said, we still hesitate. Sure, David had Jonathan, and Esther had Mordecai, and I'd love to have a cousin like Elizabeth. But what if I have no one? Or worse, what if I've tried to reach out to someone and got burned?

For every story of a Scott in my life who stood up for me, it seems I have another story of someone who stabbed me in the back emotionally. Ministry for some reason has a reputation for attracting the Judases who will betray you. I once heard "Be careful of those who idolize you, for one day they'll demonize you." Seems to hold true in many cases.

I recall leading people to Christ and seeing their lives dramatically changed for the better. Yet some of these same people only a few years later tell me I'm not deep enough for them and they are moving on to greener pastures. It's always amazing to me how quickly new Christians can become card-carrying Pharisees. Larry Osborne says in his book *Accidental Pharisees* that "becoming a Pharisee is like eating dinner at Denny's. No one plans to go there; you just end up there."[2]

One family in particular comes to mind. We were at similar stages in life and had similar interests. He had a passion for the church and our style of doing ministry. We'd eat together, read books together, and share life.

Over time I began to feel I could trust him. I'd share frustrations with him, confide in him my fears about life and ministry, and he would do the same with me. While serving as a pastor for a large church it's hard to be there for everyone, but I was there for him. When he had marriage trouble, when his kids went through surgery, and when his parents had health issues, I was there supporting him in any way I could.

My trust level for this man was so high I asked him to think about joining our board of directors. This was an invitation I don't extend often, and he was moved by the request. But somehow over the next couple of months he turned every personal trial or confession in my life into a reason *not* to be a part of the board. In fact, he decided to leave the church altogether.

After this kind of experience, how does anyone find the courage to trust again? How can I sit across from a newfound friend who loves our ministry and not be a bit gun-shy?

You've had this kind of thing happen too. A family member decides to turn on you. Or a trusted friend or colleague. Maybe even one of your children becomes rebellious and turns away. How do you find the courage to lock arms with others, circle up, and walk bravely into the dark if you don't trust the people you are closest to?

As Always, Jesus Shows Us How

We often talk about Jesus going to Gethsemane to pray. He withdrew from the disciples to pour out His heart to His Father before His crucifixion. We always read this as a tribute to solitude, a testimony to time alone with God. But we forget a few key things. Yes, He withdrew, but Jesus invited three of His group to join Him. And keep in mind, if anyone could have said, "I've got this on my own," it was Jesus. He'd just sat through a meal where one betrayed Him and ran off into the night. He knew another disciple would deny Him. Yet He invites this one, Peter, to join Him in prayer in the garden. The same disciples who kept making ridiculous decisions were the ones Jesus invited to support Him in His time of agony.

Can you imagine? They've just concluded a rather interesting mealtime. Jesus washed their feet. He talked about His upcoming death. He invited them to eat of His flesh and drink His blood. And if that wasn't awkward enough, He then reveals one of them will betray Him and another will deny knowing Him.

You think you've had some difficult family dinners. I can only imagine as they were cleaning up, a couple of the disciples washing dishes had to look at each other and say, "Wow! That was something. Did you see Judas tear out of here? And what about what He told Peter?" How do you process stuff like that? Just about the time you think Jesus would storm out and say, "I've had enough of you all . . . I've got bigger things to deal with," He says, "Come with me to pray."

I'm not like that. When I'm scared, when I have a big day ahead of me, I want to be alone. Every weekend when I come to preach I don't want to talk to anyone. Don't ask me how I'm doing; don't ask me if I'm feeling good about the message. I'll tell you when I'm done delivering it. And that's just a thirty-minute message.

Jesus was about to be arrested, beaten, and then hung on a cross for six hours as He paid for the sins of the world. If anyone would have reason to look at everyone and say, "No one understands!" it was Him. But He modeled another way. We would understand if He kept His thoughts to himself, but He brings others into His struggle. He invites them (even Peter) into His most intimate time with His Father.

If we want to learn how to lock arms and walk bravely into the dark, we need to let go of some of our expectations.

Stop waiting, start walking

I often hold out on bringing others into my life because I've been hurt . . . by them. But in this case, Jesus welcomes guys who have hurt Him or will hurt Him. I have a feeling that if Judas were to return, he'd be welcomed by Jesus too.

I like how author James Bryan Smith puts it: "The gospel is good news to the broken and contrite, to the sick who are in need of a physician. We lack community in many churches precisely because we have been ashamed to admit that we are sick. Admitting the truth of who we really are is the first step to building real community."[3]

Finding others to lock arms with is not based on what they've done for you or how well they've passed the trust test. It never hurts for them to be trustworthy, loyal friends over years of experiences, but walking into the dark only requires the support of other people. They don't have to be best buds.

We often resist sharing our fears because we think, *Who could ever understand what I'm going through? After all, no one else has blended a family, buried a father, and lost a job all in the same year.* Or have they?

Every year we start new small groups at our church, and I'm always amazed at how God puts people together. After about three weeks of meetings, we start to hear reports like "You'll never guess what happened!" To which I think *I'll bet I can.* But I don't steal their thunder. "What happened?" We had a new person share about their child with special needs and someone else in the group is in the same situation. Or a person new to the group has been silent for weeks only to open up and share about an addiction they've been battling. Then another person chimes in and says, "Me too." It's amazing how similar our lives are when we open up to each other.

I've noticed that when we offer money management classes at the church they are filled with people who think they are the only ones struggling in this area. After a few classes people start to realize, "Hey, you're just like me!" That's what happened with us. We needed to know others felt as we did so we could lock arms, circle up, and walk bravely into the darkness.

We see the same thing with marriage classes. For years I would stand up and talk about how every couple in our church should go through a class we called Marriage 101. One day it occurred to me that my wife and I had never been through that class. Our marriage seemed fine, but it could always be better. And what better way to promote the class than to actually attend it?

So Lorrie and I signed up. We even invited another couple to come with us. Their marriage was a mess, so they really needed it. *We of course did not.*

But after a few weeks I found myself taking some notes. For a friend, of course. I found Lorrie and I talking about some issues together that we'd always known about but never addressed. Looking around the room, I could see the nods of recognition with each issue discussed, and it made me feel less crazy. Less like I was on an island, all alone. We can all face our fears when we lock arms, circle up . . . .

But as great as all those experiences are, they are not a prerequisite for finding community. After all, no one—I repeat—NO ONE—could identify with what Jesus was going through. If Jesus were to say in the garden of Gethsemane, "I'm just a little preoccupied with the fact that I'm about to be arrested, falsely accused, deserted by all my friends, beaten, flogged, and crucified to pay for the sins of the world," no one would or could say, "Been there!" or "I know what you mean. I once went three days without catching a fish. Hard times!" No one understood what Jesus was going through. Yet He still longed for the presence and prayers of His friends, the disciples.

In my early days of ministry, I served at a church that included a large senior adult demographic that often found themselves in the hospital. This required someone from the church staff to visit the hospitals every day. So when it was my day, I'd make my way through the halls, stopping in to see everyone on my list. I felt like a doctor making his rounds.

But once I got to the room, I realized I'd never been trained on bedside manner. Sometimes I'd talk for thirty minutes only to discover I had the wrong bed. And nothing beats walking in on someone using the bedpan. I asked one of our older and wiser pastors on staff the basics of a good hospital visit.

He assured me that people only want two things, and in the end these are the only two things people will remember: your presence and prayer. They'll remember that you were there in their time of suffering and that you prayed for them. In the end, that's all any of us want. To know that we are not alone. And someone is praying for us. That's what Jesus wanted. Perhaps this is the way we lock arms and walk bravely into the dark . . . together.

Discussion Questions

1. What were some of your fears growing up?
2. "We all live with certain fears, and they come in all shapes and sizes." Which of the examples given can you relate to more? The monsters of regret, the clowns of finances and debt, or the haunted houses of the unknown?
3. In what ways have you addressed these problems? How can you continue, or start to, right now?
4. What are some other things that keep us from "locking arms with others, circling up, and walking bravely into the dark"?
5. What was the significance of Jesus' washing His disciples' feet, even though He knew they were going to betray Him?
6. What false expectation do we put on living in community?

Section 3

Better Together . . . to Overcome Our Weaknesses

Healing happens together

In his book *Outliers*, Malcolm Gladwell investigates a town of immigrants who left Roseto, Italy, in the 1880s and 1890s to come to America. Most of these people settled in one area of Pennsylvania, which they eventually named after the town they came from in the Old World.[1]

The new Roseto looked very much like the original. Everyone in it spoke Italian, and in the early 1900s it was a little island unto itself. In the 1950s, a doctor in the region commented to a researcher that he rarely found anyone from that area who suffered from heart disease. At that time, there were many people researching this disease, so this fact presented a mystery worth investigating. This was before cholesterol-lowering drugs, so many men in the country were dying at a young age because of heart disease.

As the research was done, they discovered this little community's population had staggeringly healthy hearts. The heart disease in men was shockingly low compared to the surrounding area and national averages. The team researched the diet of these people, their exercise patterns, and all the usual suspects for heart disease. In addition to healthy hearts, the researchers found no ulcers, no suicide, no alcoholism, no drug addiction, and very little crime. Mostly, the townspeople were dying of old age.

But why? Was it due to some dietary practice from the Old World? Not necessarily. They found the people cooked with lard and ate sausages, pepperoni, eggs, sweets, and anchovies. In fact, 41 percent of their calories were from fat. And no one was exercising.

Perhaps it was just genetics, they thought. So they tracked down other relatives who lived elsewhere to confirm, but they found that they did not have the same results. Maybe it was the climate? Only problem was, the neighboring towns did not have the same results.

To the researchers' surprise, there were no dietary behaviors or normal health patterns that surfaced to indicate why the people of Roseto were so healthy. They finally concluded it was not a physical dynamic. It was something they never expected: They lived in community.

These people lived in such a close-knit community with one another that their togetherness literally overcame their poor diets and lack of exercise. Though they ate poorly by dietary standards, they ate together. Though they were sedentary, they sat together. These people were truly better together. I don't know about you, but if I can eat Italian food all day and remain healthy, I may investigate moving to Roseto!

The healing benefit of community is an idea easily overlooked, yet hard to ignore. Robert Putnam wrote about this in his seminal work on community called *Bowling Alone*. He cites that joining a club or a group is so helpful for your health that you actually cut your odds of dying over the next year in half. And if you join two groups, your odds are cut by three-quarters. In fact, joining a group of people is likened to quitting smoking.[2] So the conclusion is, if you're going to smoke, smoke in a group!

Healing of Soul and Body

While science may show us the value of community for our health, the truth is we need deeper healing than just our bodies. I'm not even referring to sin. Jesus took care of the penalty and punishment for our sin. I'm referring to life—our soul—our ability to operate in this world.

Throughout church history, people have seen the power of community. It did more than just occupy time or advance a cause—it actually could bring healing to both body and soul.

Basil of Caesarea was the Greek bishop of the fourth century in modern-day Turkey. He is known as an early developer of Christian monasticism and the author of some of the church's earliest prayers beyond Scripture. He initially left the world to join the monastery, but eventually brought the monastery back to the world through his city of Basiliad, which was also called "The New City." This was a giant community of men and women, working with doctors and other laypeople to provide food, clothing, shelter, and medical care to the poor of Caesarea. By withdrawing from the monastic community he knew, Basil ended up establishing a broader community.

Marcella of Rome was born in AD 325 to a prominent Roman family. Less than a year after she was married, her husband died. She inherited all his wealth (including a mansion), but through the tragedy she chose to convert the mansion into one of the earliest communities for women, where she and others used their riches to help the poor.

She said she preferred to "store her money in the stomachs of the needy than hide it in a purse." In 410 the Goths invaded Rome. When they broke into the mansion and demanded money, Marcella responded that she had given it all away. She died from their beatings and torture, but her attackers were reportedly shamed by her piety before her death. "By heaven's grace, captivity has found me a poor woman, not made me one. Now I shall go in want of daily bread, but I shall not feel hunger since I am full of Christ." She found healing from her suffering by bringing others in.

J. R. R. Tolkien wrote about this in his classic anthology *The Lord of the Rings*. Frodo was healed by community, and eventually it was what prompted him to leave as well. Sam was then healed by community. His relationship with Frodo continues through Rosie and their family, and he becomes mayor of The Shire.

Speaking of Tolkien, C. S. Lewis credits his spiritual healing to a community of friends that included Tolkien and Hugo Dyson. Though Lewis was raised in the Church of Ireland, he became an atheist and only through his friends did he come back to faith.

Lewis writes about this in his book *Surprised by Joy*: "You must picture me alone in that room in Magdalen [College, Oxford], night after night, feeling, whenever my mind lifted even for a second from my work, the steady, unrelenting approach of Him whom I so earnestly desired not to meet. That which I greatly feared had at last come upon me. In the Trinity Term of 1929, I gave in, and admitted that God was God, and knelt and prayed: perhaps, that night, the most dejected and reluctant convert in all England."[3]

Bishop Dom Helder Camara, "the red bishop" of Brazil, writes, "To walk alone is possible, but the good walker knows that the great trip is life and it requires companions."[4]

Perhaps the reason we still struggle with the ailments of anxiety, self-doubt, and a quick temper has more to do with our lack of community than our lack of self-control.

But Wait . . .

Though we might achieve healing from pain by being with people, often the cause of the pain in the first place is people. Someone has hurt us, someone has burned us, and we've vowed, "Never trust again," even if healing is the goal.

While reaching out to connect with others may be humiliating or even scary, the payoff is always greater. Being better together may start with a plunge into the unknown abyss of awkward and uncomfortable social interaction, but the results can be profoundly beneficial.

Jean Vanier, founder of L'Arche federation of communities, wrote this gem:

> Almost everyone finds their early days in a community ideal. It all seems perfect. They feel they are surrounded by saints, heroes, or at the least, most exceptional people who are everything they want to be themselves. And then comes the letdown. The greater their idealization of the community at the start, the greater the disenchantment. If people manage to get through this second period, they come to a third phase—that of realism and of true commitment. They no longer see other members of the community as saints or devils, but as people—each with a mixture of good and bad, darkness and light, each growing and each with their own hope. The community is neither heaven nor

hell, but planted firmly on earth, and they are ready to walk in it, and with it. They accept the community and the other members as they are; they are confident that together they can grow toward something more beautiful."[5]

Healing through Friends

In chapter 4, we discussed the encounter between Jesus and the paralytic as told in Mark 2. Even if he wanted to find Jesus and seek healing, he was unable to get to Him on his own. In fact, were it not for his friends, he may have never found healing or salvation.

> While he was preaching God's word to them, four men arrived carrying a paralyzed man on a mat. They couldn't bring him to Jesus because of the crowd, so they dug a hole through the roof above his head. Then they lowered the man on his mat, right down in front of Jesus. Seeing their faith, Jesus said to the paralyzed man, "My child, your sins are forgiven." But some of the teachers of religious law who were sitting there thought to themselves, "What is he saying? This is blasphemy! Only God can forgive sins!" Jesus knew immediately what they were thinking, so he asked them, "Why do you question this in your hearts? Is it easier to say to the paralyzed man 'Your sins are forgiven,' or 'Stand up, pick up your mat, and walk'? So I will prove to you that the Son of Man has the authority on earth to forgive sins." Then Jesus turned to the paralyzed man and said, "Stand up, pick up your mat, and go home!" And the man jumped up, grabbed his mat, and walked out through the stunned onlookers. They were all amazed and praised God, exclaiming, "We've never seen anything like this before!"
>
> Mark 2:2–12

This is a phenomenal story of someone who was healed simply because of his friends. John Ortberg in his book *Everybody's Normal Till You Get to Know Them* refers to the incident as the "Fellowship of the Mat." These men gathered around the mat and helped the man find healing by helping him find Jesus.[6]

Healing That Restores

In Mark 5, we read about a woman who had a serious medical issue.

> A woman in the crowd had suffered for twelve years with constant bleeding. She had suffered a great deal from many doctors, and over the years she had spent everything she had to pay them, but she had gotten no better. In fact, she had gotten worse.
>
> Mark 5:25–26

She had spent twelve years visiting doctors, paying a fortune for their help, yet to no avail. This problem no doubt limited her interaction with family and friends. In those days, hygiene wasn't so easy to manage as it is today with our ready access to running water; she would have had an odor, she would have felt embarrassed, and by temple law she would have been considered unclean. Being "unclean" meant she'd not been able to go to the temple to pray for twelve years. So she experienced not only a physical discomfort but also a spiritual distance. She was in desperate need of healing.

We find her throwing caution to the wind as she approaches Jesus. The courage it would have taken her to get that far is unimaginable. Perhaps she'd simply come to the end of her rope. How long would that have taken? Two years? Five years?

How many visits to doctors had she made? How many holidays had she endured without the company of family?

She'd probably gotten used to solitude. Meet recluses and painfully shy introverts and you find people who still crave some level of human interaction but they've lost the ability and skills to connect. What do you say? How do you carry on a conversation? They wonder, *What are people really thinking when they look at me?*

You can imagine this woman's fear and desperation as she made her way through the crowd that day. She'd heard the miracle worker was coming. News of His arrival always made its way around the lakeside towns of Galilee. "He's coming! He's coming!" Could this be her opportunity? Could He help? She's not even asking the bigger question: "Is He the Messiah?" She just wants to know if He can help her with her constant isolating problem. The problem that robbed her of her freedom. The problem that separated her from God and her community. Could He fix that?

You can feel her stress as she prepares to go out in public. She likely washed her clothes, perhaps changed her appearance to distract from who she was known to be . . . unclean. She waited inside until she heard the crowds. "He's here!" "There He is!"

She slipped out of her house and made her way to the mob of people surrounding Jesus. Just as she gets there, someone gets His attention and says, "My little girl is dying . . . please come quick!" And Jesus begins to follow him.

"Is that all it takes?" she wonders. "Who is this man? I can't travel with this crowd all the way to find this little girl. By then someone will find me out. The last thing I want is more shame! Perhaps He's so powerful that if I just touch His clothes I'll be healed. After all, this rabbi is wearing a robe with dangling tassels, tassels that indicate who He is and what He's about.

These must have some sort of spiritual benefit. Perhaps they are miraculous. I have to do something."

So she lunges out to touch Him.

> She had heard about Jesus, so she came up behind him through the crowd and touched his robe. For she thought to herself, "If I can just touch his robe, I will be healed." Immediately the bleeding stopped, and she could feel in her body that she had been healed of her terrible condition.
>
> Mark 5:27–29

I love how quickly the healing happens. "Immediately." She got her miracle, and it required no prayer, no confession, no promise of repentance. Just faith . . . and risk. Just as she's about to head home, Jesus won't let her go.

> Jesus realized at once that healing power had gone out from him, so he turned around in the crowd and asked, "Who touched my robe?" His disciples said to him, "Look at this crowd pressing around you. How can you ask, 'Who touched me?'" But he kept on looking around to see who had done it.
>
> Mark 5:30–32

The disciples are a bit stunned by Jesus' question. "Are you kidding? You're in a mosh pit. *Everyone* is touching you." But Jesus knows the touch of the desperate. He knows this is different, and He won't let her get a drive-through healing. He requires that the unknown be made known.

> Then the frightened woman, trembling at the realization of what had happened to her, came and fell to her knees in front of him and told him what she had done. And he said to her,

"Daughter, your faith has made you well. Go in peace. Your suffering is over."

Mark 5:33–34

I wonder sometimes if her suffering would have returned if she'd run off and not actually addressed Jesus' question. But one thing is for sure: The suffering Jesus healed her from was not only her physical problem but also her social and spiritual isolation. Jesus seems to dig at the wound of shame just a bit so true healing can begin. Her suffering is over. She can go in peace. She can go and be with others.

Author and psychologist Brené Brown points out:

> Owning our story can be hard but not nearly as difficult as spending our lives running from it. Embracing our vulnerabilities is risky but not nearly as dangerous as giving up on love and belonging and joy—the experiences that make us the most vulnerable. Only when we are brave enough to explore the darkness will we discover the infinite power of our light.[7]

Healing through Freedom

In the letter to the Hebrews, the author reminds us that together we can find healing from all that holds us back in this race of life we are running: "Let us strip off every weight that slows us down, especially the sin that so easily trips us up. And let us run with endurance the race God has set before us" (Hebrews 12:1). Let us strip off every weight that slows us down? What is that weight? It is referred to as an entanglement, or whatever hinders us, but the image is you are running a race and you keep tripping on your shoestrings or your coat that hangs too low. Maybe this is like the ankle weights that were the craze of the

1980s for runners. In any case, the image reminds us that whatever holds us back needs to be stripped off for our own good.

It isn't just sin. Sin was paid for at the cross. Jesus took that penalty. Rather, it's our brokenness, the issues we deal with on a daily basis. The things that get in the way of our growth in Christ and keep us from becoming mature disciples. Hurts, habits, hang-ups.

These are the things that also keep us from authentic relationships. They cause us to limp our way through life. And yet these are the things that community can heal. Medical research testifies that community *may* work to heal your body, but it definitely *will* bring healing to your weary soul.

Healing in Helping Others

In all our efforts to find healing for ourselves, or in asking God to heal us or others, we forget that God may want to use *us* to help bring healing to others.

Author and speaker Dr. Tony Campolo tells the story of being at a banquet sponsored by a Christian women's organization. Before he was scheduled to speak, the leader of the event told a heartrending story of a missionary who was in need of four thousand dollars. She then looked at him and said, "Dr. Campolo, will you pray for this missionary, that God would grant his request?"

Both the leader and the audience were a bit shocked when he replied, "No." You could feel the tension rise in the room. Then he continued, "No, I won't pray for God to meet the needs of this missionary. But I'll tell you what I will do. I'll give every dime of cash I have in my pockets and place it on the table. I'm asking each of you to do the same. If we don't have the four thousand dollars, I'll pray for God to meet the need."

Somewhat reluctantly three hundred people emptied their wallets and purses. The amount raised was well over four thousand dollars. Tony then concluded, "We didn't need to pray that God would provide the resources. They were already there. We had to pray to let them go."[8]

We are not unlike the people in this story. We pray for God to meet someone else's need so we can get back to dealing with our own. After all, we don't need the burden of helping others with their pain. We have enough of our own. But sometimes God wants to use us to bring healing to others.

We have all the resources we need for the healing, but not always the willingness to share. Sometimes the resources we can provide are financial, but sometimes they are physical. Simply being with someone, walking them through chemo or a rough day, bringing someone a meal . . . all of these gestures not only help bring healing to others but bring healing to us as well.

How to Come Together . . . Better

Let others in on our pain

In order for others to run with us, they need to know which leg is bothering us, making us limp. They need to know our pain and we need to know theirs.

One of my favorite images of this type of healing is from the 1992 Olympic Games in Barcelona, Spain. It was the four-hundred-meter event in track and field, and Derek Redmond from Great Britain was heavily favored to win the gold. Derek had trained and competed for years prior to this. As he stood at the starting line, preparing for the race, he was literally four hundred meters away from making the finals.

The gun went off and so did he. He was moving at a great pace when he came around the backstretch only to feel a sharp pain in his leg. His hamstring had torn. He instantly fell to the ground in agony. After a few moments in pain, he knew his Olympic dream of winning the event was over. Olympic officials ran out to help him off the track, but he waved them off. He wanted to finish the race. He stood up in pain and began to stumble toward the finish line.

The pain was beginning to win the battle, and he found himself struggling to even take a step. As he pressed on, someone got up from his seat and made his way out of the stands and onto the track. As this person approached, Derek started to wave him off . . . until he saw who it was. He surrendered and collapsed into his father's arms. Arm in arm they walked the last hundred meters together to cross the finish line.

It would be easy to let this story remind us that our heavenly Father has come down out of heaven to run our race with us. But it speaks of more than that. As the book of Hebrews points out (12:1), we have a cloud of witnesses running with us in life. We are only as alone as we want to be.

Discussion Questions

1. If there is so much scientific data on the benefits of living in close community, why do we continue to insist on living individually and alone?

2. If we're saved, we often see the soul as the only part of us that floats off to heaven when we die. How do our bodies *and* souls play significant roles in our overall well-being in the present?

3. How do you think our society would look if we actually began to model the examples of community that were highlighted in this chapter?

4. There is a powerful quote by Jean Vanier in this chapter, in which he describes various levels in regard to living in true community. Go back and read the quote. What level would you say you're at right now?

5. Almost all of Jesus' healings connected the physical with the spiritual and restored people into right relationship with others around them. How does the physical and spiritual correlate when it comes to living in community? Why do you think Jesus chose to highlight this?

6. As was mentioned, gestures of healing and service in community don't only heal others, they bring healing to ourselves as well. Have you ever thought about that? What are some things that "tangle you up" and inhibit your potential to impact others?

7. "In order for others to run with us, they need to know which leg is bothering us . . ." What are some ways you can be more open in order to invite others into your life on a daily basis?

8

Temptations
are conquered together

Everyone has a story of a mistake they made as a kid that they tried to hide. For me, it was a framed picture I broke in our house. I was doing the unthinkable—kicking a soccer ball inside, something I'd been told not to do because I might break something. But I was tempted. After all, the ball was just sitting there on the floor, and it was raining outside. So I began to slightly and ever so carefully kick it around the room and off the walls. Nothing broke, so I was clearly very good at this. So I kept it up. Of course, just as I began to get confident . . . smash!

I was horrified. I knew I was in big trouble, so my solution was simple. Get rid of the evidence. I scooped up the glass and carefully placed it in the trash can. I even tried to heap other trash on top of it to shield it from view. But the one thing I missed was this: *There was a bare spot on the wall*. It was pretty obvious the picture was gone. I failed to think that one through. And needless to say, I was in trouble. I wish I could say that was the last time I was tempted to break the rules, but it seems to be a common occurrence.

It's funny how kids refer to these incidents as "I was in trouble." It's clear there are consequences for our actions, but the quicker we deal with them, the quicker they're over. No more hiding, worrying, wondering if someone will find out. It's so much easier to just come clean.

As we grow up we stop using terms like *trouble* or even *temptation* and say things like "I have a weakness for (fill in the blank)" or "This is just my guilty pleasure." The problem with that approach is this: Weaknesses can turn into habits, and guilty pleasures can turn into addictions. What happens in Vegas doesn't always stay in Vegas. And what happened on the business trip always comes home with us. These decisions impact our relationships, produce extreme guilt, and more often than not they cause us to hide out. When we ignore trouble—it usually finds us.

I'm reminded of the story of Adam and Eve in the garden of Eden. They lived in complete peace and intimacy with each other and with God, yet after they sinned—they hid. They hid their bodies from each other and they hid themselves from the presence of God. How could one even do that . . . hide from God? But they tried. And so do we.

Granted, we are not ten years old, trying to cover up a broken picture. That would be a bit easier to deal with. The last thing we want to do when we are faced with temptation is to talk about it. There's a sense of being weaker than everyone else. No one wants to be sitting poolside with their neighbors and bring up their lust for someone across the pool. No mom picking up her kids from school wants to admit she's tempted to drink all day when the kids are in class. So we keep quiet.

When we're faced with group settings, where we can be vulnerable, we cover up our shortcomings by only sharing things like "I yelled at the kids" or "I'm overworked." Most of our Bible study groups can be exhausting as we try to keep struggles concealed while propping up our acts of goodness.

The only thing worse than the thought of confessing our temptations would be to reveal how we've given in to them. No one wants to share that they actually did drink all day while the kids were at school and then slept through the pickup. Or how they've been flirting with the neighbor and actually had a one-night stand on a business trip. Why bring it up if no one will understand? Or worse, judge you. So we conclude, *I'll just fix it on my own and one day share the story of how I overcame it. After all, "I can do all things through Christ who strengthens me."* But what if the way Christ strengthens us is by sharing it with others?

Healing through Sharing Our Loads

In the classic story from Edgar Allan Poe, *The Tell-tale Heart,* we read of a man who took the life of another and hid him beneath the floorboards. The guilt he felt began to manifest itself in the sound of a beating heart coming from beneath the floor of his house. Could his friend still be alive? Could his heart be that loud? Could others hear it? Of course not, but the secret he kept was a noise that could not be drowned out with the life he tried to live. He eventually turned himself in to stop the madness.

Why are the secrets we try so hard to keep the ones we most desperately need someone to help us carry? I'm reminded of the less-than-profound original campy Batman film from 1966. Why I remember these things, I don't know. But in the film, Batman has found a live bomb. Nothing fancy, just the standard bowling ball with a wick. The wick is obviously burning, and apparently no one can find a way to just put it out, so Batman is forced to pick it up and run, looking for a place to throw it. The problem is, everywhere he goes he finds more people . . . a marching band, a lovestruck couple, even a flock of ducks. Exasperated, he finally stops and shouts, "Some days you just can't get rid of a bomb!"

Most days you can't get rid of your worst secret, and you don't want to. So you carry it with you, hoping that someday someone will help you shoulder the load.

The brother of Jesus seemed to have a take on this. James, one of the contributors to the Bible, was not one of the initial disciples. He was a non-believer in Jesus until after the resurrection. That makes sense to me. It would take my resurrection for my sister to believe her brother was the Son of God. James comes to faith after this event and spends the rest of his life telling people that his brother was the Messiah.

Think about the guilt he would have carried. *All those years I doubted, all those times I thought He was crazy. All those weaknesses and temptations, and the sin I carried around, hoping the blood of bulls and goats would make me right with God. And all the while God himself was sharing a room with me. How could I have missed it? What do I do now?*

James writes a letter to a group of Jesus followers, telling them how to endure suffering and persecution as well as how to live in unity with each other. Some of our most quoted material from the New Testament is found in his letter. Toward the end of it he gives some shocking advice: "Confess your sins to each other and pray for each other so that you may be healed" (James 5:16).

I know we all push back on that with this loophole: "Can't I just confess my sins to Jesus?" After all, 1 John 1:9 says I can: "But if we confess our sins to him, he is faithful and just to forgive us our sins and to cleanse us from all wickedness." That's true. But the James reference doesn't refer to confessing our sins to Jesus.

I went to lunch one day with a friend. He's part of the church, I've known him for years, and meeting with him never seemed like business or pastoral work. We were just friends hanging out. We enjoyed a leisurely lunch and lots of laughs, catching up about family and work.

As we walked to the car I remarked to him, "I love having lunch with you—I never feel I'm on the clock having to fix you." To which he replied, "Now that you mention it, I do need to talk to you about something." I thought, *Oh great, I spoke too soon!*

He began to share a personal temptation with pornography and how he occasionally gave in to that temptation. I could see the pain and shame on his face as he told me, but I could also feel the weight being lifted as he told me. I was not working. I was not on the clock, with a task to fix him. I was helping a friend find healing just by listening. No longer was he carrying this on his own. He was being healed. We talked about setting up a program on his computer that would alert me by email about any questionable sites he was viewing. No longer would he be on his own. He had accountability.

I preached a message one weekend about forgiveness. In doing so, I spent a good deal of time on this James passage. All of us should find someone to share our secrets with, I urged the congregation. A woman came up to me afterward and asked, "Can't I forgive someone and not tell anyone?" I said, "Yes, but you won't be healed."

In many ways Alcoholics Anonymous has created this kind of healing environment. They have formed a community that is bound by their weaknesses. It started as a discipleship program, and slowly the founders began to see that people were getting sober as a result. This is why at the conclusion of their meetings they repeat together, "Keep coming back. It works!" And it does.

Bringing Temptations into the Light

James Bryan Smith shares a powerful story of being on a two-day retreat with some pastors and church leaders. On the final evening, they decided to have a Communion service, and one of the leaders suggested offering an opportunity for people to come for a private prayer of anointing, to let them share any hurts or confess any sins.

> I said, "Do you think anyone will come? I mean, these are all church leaders. I can't imagine they would want to do this."
>
> That evening nearly everyone at the retreat came for a time of private confession. I had no idea they were struggling, as I am sure they had no idea I was fighting and losing internal battles as well. Our faces never betrayed us. They shared their shortcomings and faults, their past mistakes and present demons, sometimes in detail, and I simply listened. Then I anointed their foreheads with oil in the sign of the cross and announced their forgiveness. One of them offered the same opportunity for me, and I was able to bring some things to the light with which I had been struggling.
>
> Our faces looked different after that time. They shined. Later that night I thought of how all of us—literally all of us—struggle with sin. One thing was strange: even though I could remember their faces, I could not remember their sins. I supposed God couldn't either.

Earlier, Smith writes: "We lack community in many churches precisely because we have been ashamed to admit that we are sick. Admitting the truth of who we really are is the first step to building real community."[1]

John Ortberg writes in *Soul Keeping*:

> Habits eat willpower for breakfast. No matter all the willpower you muster up, if your habits don't change, you won't change. If you create a New Year's Resolution to lose 20 pounds but keep buying Oreos, you're going to struggle. Jesus taught us to pray by saying, "Lead us not into temptation" but as much as we pray that, if we don't change our habits, we'll keep walking into temptation and then either blaming God for not leading us away or blame ourselves for not having enough willpower."[2]

In his letter, James defines the cycle of temptation we all get stuck in:

> Each person is tempted when they are dragged away by their own evil desire and enticed. Then, after desire has conceived, it gives birth to sin; and sin, when it is full-grown, gives birth to death.
>
> James 1:14–15 NIV

This is the cycle of our habits. Our habits of feeding our evil desires keep providing opportunities for our temptations. If it's our habits that keep us stuck, what are the habits that empower our temptations?

The habit of going inward

Most of us are tempted to just suppress whatever our issues are and assume no one else would ever understand. Look again at what James tells us the root cause of our temptation is: our evil desires.

Our temptations are individual things—prompted by our own desires. What tempts me may not tempt you. Here's how Eve's desires led her to sin: "When the woman saw that the fruit of the tree was good for food and pleasing to the eye, and also desirable for gaining wisdom, she took some and ate it" (Genesis 3:6 NIV).

All of us struggle with this. We think we can meet our needs better and sometimes quicker than God can. For Eve, she saw something pleasing to the eye and a way to gain wisdom. For Adam, the temptation may have been to keep peace in the family at all costs. Whatever it was, their desires (and ours) are unique and often they separate us from each other.

Look at the next step in James 1: The evil desire drags us away and entices us.

The nature of temptation is to separate us from one another. Especially from those who do not partake. Ultimately temptation separates us from God.

It is then that sin happens. These desires give birth to sinful actions. And when sin is allowed to grow, it gives birth to death.

The sin is not in the temptation; it is in the acting upon it, giving in to it. In between temptation and sin is isolation.

If our temptation, which is unique and normal, drives us away from other people, could the remedy be to run toward community?

The habit of creating chaos

One of the ways we respond to our temptation is to own it and let it define us. We yell things like "This is who I am. Just deal with it!" "I have an anger problem, okay?" "I'm my mother's son!" or "I'm Italian!" Whatever it is, sometimes we get so comfortable with our weaknesses we just own them and let them wreak havoc on everyone in our path. It's almost as if by drawing attention to it, we beat everyone else to the punch.

Years ago, I was leading a Bible study with a group of young adults. Every week a hundred of them (ages twenty-five to forty-five) would gather to talk about the Bible, sing together, and, of course, eat snacks. As the Scripture says, "Where two or more are gathered, there will be nachos."

This gathering would get into a rut sometimes with the mundane nature of meeting, eating, and leaving. So every now and then I'd try to shake it up a bit. One night I had the great idea of teaching on sins we all struggle with. I challenged them to write their troubling sin on a piece of paper with the idea that we'd take them outside and burn them.

You have to set people up for this by having some contemplative music, dimming the lights, and reading Scripture. Many of them were struggling with sinful choices involving others *in the room*, so you had to get them to focus on what they should do about that. Forgive, stop lusting, stop manipulating, and start serving.

After what seemed like a proper time of teaching and singing, I passed out scraps of paper and pencils. Each person took their time to carefully write out their besetting sins. We marched solemnly outside and surrounded a half barrel that would serve as our sin altar. Then we all dropped our papers into the barrel. Once we were done, we prayed, and I carefully and thoughtfully took out a lighter and lit the mound of paper scraps. Slowly the "sin fire" took off and billowed smoke and sparks into the night sky. People were moved. Some began to cry. Others just stared as their longtime addictions, unresolved grudges, and destructive habits were consumed by holy fire.

It was during this worship event that someone slowly emerged from the crowd, someone I'd just met that night. He walked past everyone, including me, and knelt by the fire. Was he going to pray? No, he took out a cigarette and proceeded to try to light it off the sin fire.

People were horrified. Some had no doubt written *smoking* on their paper. Others felt he was making a mockery of our solemn act. A few were just amused watching him try to light a cigarette from a raging fire. This proved too difficult because the flames were rather unpredictable.

So he walked over to me and put out his hand. Still stunned, I started to shake his hand, but he said, "No, give me your lighter." I couldn't think of anything else to do so I handed him the lighter. It was clear that smoking was a habit he needed and maybe wanted to break, but he also clearly had a habit of making a scene. When attention trumps assistance, you'll always be left in need.

The habit of selective disclosure

I find that when I want to be vulnerable, I often pick different people to confide in. If I want to talk about my struggle with jealousy over the success of another church, I'll call up a pastor friend of mine and tell him. After commiserating, we begin to find reasons why others are more successful than we are—all because they sold out—and none of it has to do with us. Confession can turn into gossip and then slander.

But I don't confess this kind of thing to my wife. After all, she wouldn't understand. And she may tell me to stop taking myself too seriously. (Clearly she doesn't understand how important I am.)

If I'm struggling with my kids, I tell my wife. She knows the difficulties. She can commiserate. If I were to tell a friend in our small group, he might tell me to do something about it. So over the course of a few years, everyone can know a part of me, but no one really knows me. This feels like I'm being vulnerable, but I'm actually controlling what others think of me.

What if we learned some new habits with our temptations? If confession brings healing, and we need healing, let's look at what habits might help us share our personal temptations with each other.

How to Come Together . . . Better

Be honest with at least a few

Instead of trying to be partially honest with everyone, be fully honest with a few. I'm not saying to lie to the rest. I'm just saying that levels of transparency are helpful. The danger comes when we are only partially honest with everyone. Then no one really knows us, and therefore no one can really help us.

I might think, *I can tell this person; after all, he's worse than I am.* Or *I will tell him one thing because I think he'll be sympathetic. And then I'll tell her something else, because it will be unifying.* In our effort to break temptation we leverage control.

In one of my first men's Bible studies I ever led, I saw an example of this that I've carried with me ever since. We were all around the age of twenty-five. I was the only one married at the time, but we spent a great deal of time talking about relationships. I remember going home from that group many nights thinking, *I'm not sure we are getting past the surface. Everyone seems to be holding back.*

I knew these guys had struggles, but no one was talking. Until one night, when the floodgates opened. It all started with one person. We were about to close up for the night, when one guy spoke up and said, "I had sex with my girlfriend last night."

The silence was deafening for about five seconds. "I felt really bad about it and wanted to tell you guys," he added.

I asked, "How'd she feel?" To which he jokingly said, "She felt great to me!" I'm not saying we were the most mature group of guys. But it did bring a bit of levity to the room. Someone else said, "Okay, thanks for telling us. Here's what we're going to do. We're going to ask you every week if you two have been abstaining. Maybe knowing we are going to ask will help you have some accountability." He said, "That would be great."

Then another guy in our group said, "Well, since we're confessing, I'd like to stop drinking, but I just keep buying it." To which someone else said, "Okay, everyone take something out of their wallet that is unique to them." He collected various pictures and cards, then said to the guy who'd confessed his struggle, "Now, put these in your wallet. Every time you go to buy alcohol, you'll see us looking at you!" His response? "That sounds great!"

Then another guy spoke up: "Well, now that you guys have shared . . . I'm trying to quit smoking." (No, it wasn't the guy from the sin fire!) To which another guy said, "Been there. Here's what you do. Get a bunch of those atomic fireball candies and just pop those in your mouth when you want to smoke. That hot sensation on the back of your throat is enough to curb that craving."

After that night, I'd see that individual from the platform where I was teaching and he'd be popping fireballs. It always made me laugh—thinking of him taking a drag while in church. That night in small group we laughed, we prayed, we encouraged, and oddly enough, when we left there that night, all of us were carrying each other's burdens. Yet all of us felt lighter.

Discussion Questions

1. What was the biggest mistake you made as a kid and tried to hide? Did you get away with it? Ever tell on yourself?

2. We often ridicule Adam and Eve for trying to hide from God, but we do the same thing. What are the most common excuses you use in order to minimize or hide the things in your life you know to be sinful? (Example: "I don't talk to anyone because I'm an introvert.")

3. The author asks, "Why are the secrets we try so hard to keep the ones we most desperately need someone to help us carry?" How would you answer this question?

4. Have you ever participated in any sort of group confession? What is the importance of confession for living in true community together?

5. Why do you think it is important that forgiveness sometimes be a public act? What's the harm in "forgiving and not telling"?

6. What is the connection between habits and temptations? How can we create new habits in order to address the temptations we have in life and connect us to community in a stronger way?

7. "Instead of trying to be partially honest with everyone, be fully honest with a few." Do you have people in your life you can be perfectly honest with? If so, list them. If not, make a list of potential people and approach them to see if they may be open to this level of honesty with you, and you with them.

Perfectionists
find peace together

As great as Easter services can be for the church, they are particularly exhausting for the staff. So when a sweet couple came up to me one year prior to Easter and offered a relaxing getaway for me and my family the Monday after Easter, I was thrilled. My mind was racing with what that might be: a resort on the beach? A cabin in the mountains? I was not expecting their answer: A trip to Disneyland.

To be perfectly honest, I was grateful but at the same time I dreaded it. The crowds, the heat, and the pressure to accomplish everything—it sounded like another Easter service. It was at this point they said, "Now, I know what you're thinking." I thought, *I'm not sure you do.* They continued, "We want to give you a VIP tour." Then I thought, *I know my way around Disneyland. I've been there a few times and I can read the map.*

But they said, "A VIP tour gets you to the front of the line of every ride you want to take."

"Tell me more," I said. "The VIP tour provides you with a tour guide who is basically your human FastPass. They take you to the front of every line. The only problem is this will ruin you on Disneyland." I said, "I'm okay with that!"

When I told our kids, they were ecstatic. So was my wife. And to be honest, so was I.

The thought of being led through the park and escorted to the front of every line seemed like a dream. Finally we would be those people we used to despise, the ones who walked past us with their FastPasses or fancy wristbands—the ones who "knew someone" or had "special privileges." We were about to be the VIPs!

The day after Easter, we made the hour-long drive down to Disneyland. We followed the instructions we'd been given and walked up to the VIP meeting spot. Sure enough, there was a young man with a very official vest and name badge waiting for us.

"Are you the Georges?" he asked. "Yes, we are." "Great! I'm Andrew, and I will be your human FastPass. I'll get you to the front of every line." It was at this point that my oldest daughter, Lindsey, pulled out a sheet of paper. She said, "This is a list of rides we would like to ride today." He took a quick glance at it, folded it up, put it in his pocket, and said, "We'll get to them." I was laughing to myself about my daughter's need to control the situation. "Relax," I said to her, "we're in good hands."

But as we entered the park, I realized something I'd never experienced before—someone else had all of our tickets. He scanned them, ushered us in, and put them in *his* pocket. This was so foreign to me because I've always held the tickets. The tickets are used not only to get into the park but also to reserve spots on the rides, so I am always afraid if I don't hold onto them someone will lose their ticket.

Even scarier was the first moment I realized I wasn't in charge. Usually I lead our family through the park on a mission. "Run to Space Mountain!" "Eat while in line!" "You can go to the bathroom when we leave!" After all, you have to maximize every moment. I call it leadership. My family has other terms for it.

But as we followed Andrew into the park, I was beginning to panic. Apparently my daughter wasn't the only one with control issues. (More on this later.)

Three Things that Define Control Freaks

I've been told the reasons we control freaks struggle are simple. They boil down to three main issues.

First, everything I do must be perfect

This can look like endless Post-it Notes, to-do lists, project management, and micromanaging as well. Control freaks stay up all night stressing about how things will get done and what others will think about it. It takes us thirty minutes to post something on social media as we double- and triple-check grammar and wittiness. If I've been given a task, then I must knock it out of the park. It must be the best thing anyone has ever seen. Because if for some reason I don't get glowing reviews it will be seen as a complete failure.

I will feel this after giving a message at times. I'll stand in the lobby and hear people say the kindest things: "Great job!" "You're so good." "That was such a blessing." But in my mind I'm thinking, *Why don't others say that? They say that every week, so it doesn't count.* Or *If they said this message was my best, does that mean the others weren't any good?*

Contrary to popular belief, control freaks can also be procrastinators. Our fear of not being perfect can cause us not to even get in the game. "If I can't be perfect, then I won't even try." Or worse, "I'll self-sabotage so even *you* will stop believing in me." I've seen this in marriages, where a spouse continues with an addictive behavior for fear of not being able to stay sober. Might as well jump off the bridge with both feet and at least be right about one thing—I can't do anything right.

Second, everyone else must be perfect

It's not enough for me to put this pressure on myself; I'm going to hold you to a ridiculous standard as well. In fact, often my frustration with your imperfection is just my frustration with myself projected onto you. Because of this you must always be on time, you must always be accurate. You must never make a mistake, you must always say the right thing, and you must always live up to the standard in my mind.

This is why we control freaks have some tense moments in marriage. One person thinks, *I have expectations for what you should do for my birthday, Christmas, our anniversary. But I'll never tell you. You need to guess. And if you get it right, then I'll come up with another expectation.*

I knew I had this issue when my wife threw me a surprise party for my thirtieth birthday. The lights came on, people yelled "SURPRISE!" and in about five seconds I had done roll call in my head and had a list of who *wasn't* there and how the party would be even better if they had been. How could my wife have missed that? Sure, she invited my best friend from college and he and his family had driven three hours to be there, but didn't she know there was a U2 concert that night and several of my friends were at the concert so they couldn't attend? How exhausting this must be for everyone in our life. They keep trying to jump over a bar we keep raising.

Third, conditions must always be perfect

Most of us control freaks, or perfectionists, believe that the conditions must be perfect as well as everyone playing a role in them. When my wife and I were dating, I'd work hard for the perfect meal in the perfect restaurant with the perfect ambiance. Surely this would make for an evening only seen in movies.

But it was inevitable. Something would always go wrong. The food wouldn't be great, or the server would forget to light our candle. One of my pet peeves is no background music. If there's no music, there's no mood. Silence becomes deafening. Every moment must be like a Cary Grant movie. Violins aren't necessary, but there must be music.

Now that we are married with kids and have shared twenty-plus years of life together, you'd think I'd be over trying to make every situation perfect, but not so much. Sometimes I'll make it home before my wife and see the evidence of what looks like a hectic day. The kids have left out breakfast dishes, the dogs have strung out their toys, and the couch cushions are displaced. (I know, some of you are thinking, *I'm just happy if the dishes, toys, dogs, and cushions are in the house*, but for some of us less sane, these can be an issue.)

So I get it in my mind that I'll clean up all these things and create the perfect relaxing scenario. I straighten the cushions, pick up the toys, clean up the kitchen, and do the dishes and put them away. Then I put on her favorite music, light the candles, and start dinner. In my mind, I envision my wife saying, *"Wow! This place looks amazing! You are the greatest!"* She will look around, commenting on everything I have done with elaborate praise and thanks.

I know, probably too much to ask. What typically happens is the garage door opens and the kids run in, throwing backpacks on the floor and lunch boxes on the counter. My wife stumbles in, harried and frustrated from the traffic. And the words I hear are "Will you get the groceries out of the car?" I might be exaggerating, but you can see how my perfect scenario overlooked the human element. No one was allowed to be real.

The Impact of a Control Freak

Living with this mentality of perfection is exhausting. No one can keep up with it. It's like they are asked to play a part in a movie they've never seen and are not given a script. Then they're judged on their performance. It can make people hate to be around us. It can make us hate to be around others. It can even make us hate to be around ourselves.

The fallout is real. Perhaps you have kids who are scared of you and exhausted by you. They can't keep up with your changing expectations and high demands. Maybe you have a spouse who feels their only defense is to retreat. They stay at the office longer and get involved in more activities, and have given up on keeping up with your idea of what life should be.

The frustrating thing about all this is that this mentality also creeps into our pursuit of being Christlike. We read about the fruit of the Spirit and think, *How is that possible? How am I to add love, joy, peace, patience, kindness, goodness, self-control, gentleness, and faithfulness to my already overwhelming to-do list?*

Our solution is to perfect ourselves by perfecting others and optimizing our conditions. Surely the right setting will create joy and peace in me. And if you would act more like

I want you to, then I would be more patient and kind. But in this attempt to solve everyone's problems, we miss out on two critical pieces that enable us to experience the fruit of the Spirit in our lives.

The Holy Spirit's presence

Paul tells us: "If we live by the Spirit, let us also keep in step with the Spirit" (Galatians 5:25 ESV).

Often we are so consumed with all that we need to do to be loving, joyful, and peaceful that we forget the very Spirit of God is standing next to us waiting for us to ask for help. My guess is you've already heard that. We often hear too that to see the fruit of the Spirit in our lives we need to surrender to the Holy Spirit. But what we forget is what He uses to help us come to a place of surrender.

The Holy Spirit's power through community

Look how Paul continues: "Let us not become conceited, provoking one another, envying one another" (Galatians 5:26 ESV).

> Let us not become weary in doing good, for at the proper time we will reap a harvest if we do not give up. Therefore, as we have opportunity, let us do good to all people, especially to those who belong to the family of believers.
>
> Galatians 6:9–10 NIV

How can we become kind or good or loving if we aren't around others to be kind, good, and loving toward? How can we demonstrate kindness, gentleness, and self-control if we don't have other people challenging and testing our commitment to display these qualities?

The process of growing spiritual fruit is fortunately not dependent upon perfection: how perfect we are, how perfect the community of people around us is, or how perfect circumstances are. All that's needed is the Holy Spirit's power working in us through our interactions with others.

Fortunately Jesus models this for us.

Jesus Shows Us the Value of Imperfect Community

At one of the most celebrated and sacred moments of our faith, we have a beautiful picture of community. On the night before Jesus was crucified, He had a meal with His closest friends. We refer to this as the Last Supper or the Lord's Supper. To them, it was the Passover.

This was the most holy event on the Jewish calendar and it was also the most communal. Everything would have to be perfect. For Jesus, this was the night he'd been looking forward to for some time, His chance to tell the disciples more about who He was. It would also be their last time to eat together before the crucifixion—a night He knew they would never forget. The scene would be a memorable setting for the disciples long after He was gone. (Not to mention be the subject of one of the most famous paintings of all time.)

Have you ever had a meal you wanted to be perfect? I remember one Thanksgiving when I volunteered to roast the turkey. I had seen Bobby Flay pull it off on Food Network and it looked pretty easy, so I was quite confident. What I wasn't prepared for was all the prep. My major mistake was not in the temperature or the basting or even the time in the oven. My mistake was revealed when I chose to slice this succulent bird in front of all the guests only to discover I had failed to remove the bag containing the innards that was neatly packed in the cavity of the turkey. Bobby Flay didn't mention this.

Not everything works out perfectly. But if there should be any meal where it did, it should have been the Last Supper. But it wasn't.

First, there was no servant available to wash their feet.

Though this is unheard of today, it was customary back then. Everyone wore sandals and walked on dirt roads, so their feet were dirty. When they came inside for a meal, they needed to clean their feet. Especially for this meal, when they would be reclining around a table. Their feet would be close to the food they were going to eat. So when a foot washer didn't show up, it was a big deal.

But Jesus uses the occasion to teach His disciples about serving one another. What a great lesson it was in how facing problems is better together. Rather than focusing on who is NOT there, focus on who is. Jesus stepped up and became the servant. He wrapped a towel around His waist and went around to each person, washing his dirty feet. I have to imagine, if the disciples were anything like us, they were sitting there complaining about how there was no one there to wash their feet. Jesus leveraged a negative into a positive experience.

Second, there was a traitor at the table.

Jesus was having one of the most spiritual meals with his closest friends, and yet things weren't perfect. Not everyone was singing "Kumbaya."[1] It's believed that Judas had joined the band of disciples to be part of the overthrow of Rome. This would guarantee a position for him in the new kingdom established by Jesus. The problem was, as time went on, he could see Jesus was more concerned with a spiritual kingdom than an earthly one. Some think Judas turned Jesus in to the authorities to force His hand, to get Him to bring in a new world order. Judas may not have wanted Jesus' death, just His attention.

We don't know all of his motives, but we know one: Judas was motivated by money. He served as treasurer for the disciples and paid the bills. Once, when a woman poured out an expensive jar of perfume on Jesus, it was Judas who objected and said, in effect, "What is she doing? That could have been sold . . ." (cue everyone staring at him) ". . . and given to the poor, of course." This was the guy at the table with Jesus. Hardly perfect.

Third, Jesus had to reprimand someone.

Have you ever had your perfect dinner messed up by having to discipline one of your kids? Jesus had to speak some tough truth to one of His own at this final meal. Peter had just declared his undying devotion, and Jesus had to break the news to him that he'd deny knowing Him.

Peter displayed a wide range of emotions during this meal. When Jesus came to wash his feet, Peter said, "I can't let you do this!" To which Jesus responded, "If I don't, you have no part of me." "Oh, well, in that case, wash my feet and my head." Again Jesus corrects him, "Uh, you don't need a bath." Later, when Jesus explains what Judas is about to do, Peter reacts with "I'll never do that." Again, Jesus brings it back to reality with "You are actually going to deny me three times." Peter was just as shocked as any of us would be.

This important meal was far from perfect. The conditions weren't perfect, and other than Jesus, the participants weren't perfect, yet we are still talking about it today because it's at this table we see Jesus modeling love and gentleness for His disciples. He has joy and peace even though the cross is in sight. He is patient and faithful with God's plan for His suffering. He is kind, good, and self-controlled even to those who are about to betray and deny Him.

In a strange and powerful way this one meal teaches all of us control freaks and perfectionists that we really are better together (and nothing is perfect).

How to Find Good in the Less Than Perfect

Leverage others' gifts

While many of us perfectionists view emotional people as problems to avoid, Jesus sees more in Peter than just high drama. He sees his passion as a gifting that will help launch His church. This passion will not only protect his own skin but will also make him passionate to seek God's forgiveness. Peter's passion will give him the moxie to preach a sermon to a hostile crowd and tell them to REPENT . . . for they have just killed the Son of God.

Adding passionate people into our lives will do more than smooth out our rough edges or teach us a lesson. We can help them harness that passion or energy for something good with long-lasting benefits. Some of the best parents I know have figured out a way to parent each child toward their gifts rather than toward their own plan.

Acknowledge the imperfections

For me, the shocking thing about Judas's betrayal is not the betrayal itself but the fact that Jesus knew it was coming and still welcomed him at His table of friends. In fact, when Judas was exposed, Jesus said, "What you're about to do, do quickly." He doesn't appear to be trying to head it off or change his mind. I guess this shouldn't be shocking for us. Jesus' table was always populated by the imperfect. The Pharisees criticized Him for "eating with tax collectors and other sinners" (Mark 2:16).

Jesus models for us that everyone is welcome at His table. Do you think the disciples talked about Judas later? "How could Jesus have allowed *him* to be there? How long did He know? When did He discover what was going on? Was He ever going to expose him?" Jesus knew that allowing the imperfect at His table would be a lesson for all of us for years to come.

You see this often with parents who have kids with addictions. What will they allow? How will they set up boundaries? How will they still parent the other kids while not allowing the addict to dominate every meal, conversation, vacation, and weekend? It can get complicated.

Find a plan B

Perfectionists tend to view others as spectators to their potential failure. But shifting your perspective to see people around you as opportunities to serve can make all the difference. The absence of a foot washer could have been an opportunity to point fingers and cast blame, but Jesus used it as a chance to model servanthood.

When I think about it, most of the reasons I melt down when faced with imperfections have to do with how I think other people will view *me*. "How will this make me look? What will they think of me?" Instead, imperfections can be a great way to find another plan.

> This weekend was far from what we planned, but how can we work together to come up with a great solution?

> I didn't get the promotion, but maybe I could encourage the one who did.

> This vacation was less than perfect. But how could I have made it great for someone else?

Let's return to our Disneyland VIP tour. As we walked through the gates I was struggling to process everything. *Someone is in charge and it is not me.* Our guide Andrew led us to a ride we'd never tried before. I said, "We always start with Cars." He said, "We'll get there." We rode the ride, and it was great. Then I said, "We'd like to ride Tower of Terror." He said, "We'll get to that." We rode another ride. It was fine. I said, "How about Space Mountain?" He said, "We'll get to that." For the next three hours we walked to the front of the line of every ride. Not always the rides I wanted to ride, but everyone but me was having fun. Why couldn't I enjoy this? Conditions were perfect . . . except for the fact that I wasn't in control. We were not executing my game plan.

Finally something happened that I was actually excited about. My wife looked at me and said, "I can't find my phone." Why was I excited about this? Because finding her phone was my new mission. I was useful again. I told our tour guide about her phone being lost. He replied, "Let me make a few calls. I'll bet we can track it down."

I looked at him with determination and said, "I have an app on my phone that allows me to track the missing phone." I was a man on a mission, and more important, the man in charge. As I raced through the park, following the dot on my phone, I could see the phone's location bouncing all over the place, but I was honing in.

Just as I thought I was getting close, my phone rang. I answered, curious. "Rusty?" "Uh . . . Yes." "This is Andrew, your tour guide." "Yes?" He said, "We found your wife's phone. I made a couple of calls and a cast member found it and is taking it to the front of the park." Then he added with just a touch of frustration, "Why don't you meet us at It's a Small World *and enjoy the rest of the day?*"

I knew he was right. I needed to surrender control if I wanted to enjoy the day. I went back to the rest of my family and to Andrew with a different attitude. And guess what? I had a great time. Maybe together in community IS better.

Discussion Questions

1. Does it make you uncomfortable or relieved to know that exhibiting the fruit of the Spirit actually involves the Holy Spirit?

2. How does the Holy Spirit relate to our being "better together"?

3. From the three suggestions for finding good in the less than perfect, which one do you find most difficult? Leveraging others' giftedness, acknowledging the imperfections, or finding a plan B? Why do you think this is true?

Section 4

Better Together . . . to Leave a Legacy

Families are built to last together

By now you may be thinking: *Okay, I can do community. I have a family.*

You're a mom with three kids. You get them ready for school each day: make sure they have their homework, fix their breakfast, and make lunches to take. You give them pep talks in the car about working hard, being kind, and not forgetting anything important. You volunteer in their classroom. You pick them up after school and drive them to their activities. You cheer from the sidelines, provide snacks after practice, and rush everyone home in time to eat the meal you've planned or prepared ahead of time. You help with their homework, remind them to shower, and get them tucked into bed. You've certainly invested in a community. Check *that* off the list.

Maybe you're a family with two working parents. It's hard to accomplish all the things on the list above because you both work, but you do your best, carpooling and divvying up the shuttling of kids to their practices and games. You try to scoot out of work early to make it to after-school events, but it's tough. Many of the meals you eat as a family are in the car, courtesy of the drive-through.

So when weekends come around, you have a bunker mentality. Close the doors, shut off the phones, get the chores done, play a board game while watching a movie, or have a tea party while playing dress up. If you go out, the entire family goes—for bike rides, Little League games, and ice cream runs. The goal is to soak up as much family time as possible. Let's make up for all the hours lost by both of us working. Attend church? Maybe. A small group? You're crazy. My community is at home.

Perhaps you're a dad who sees his kids every other weekend. Your time with your kids is precious, so you try to make the most of it. You want your kids to long to be with you, to miss their time with you, and if that means going overboard with activities and fun, then so be it. Movies, dinner out, amusement parks, camping trips, whatever it takes! Community? Yep. You're on it.

Maybe you're taking care of aging parents. They require daily visits from you or they may even live with you. It seems most of your time away from your job is focused on assisting them. Between the doctor visits, meal preparation, and medicine dispensing, you are pretty busy. Your community quotient is met!

Drive home, pull in the garage, shut the door, turn off the phone, eat dinner together, do homework, say your prayers, put the kids to bed. You are investing in your family by protecting them from everything and everyone else. Playdates are scheduled. Friends are screened. And schools and churches are scrutinized to make sure we protect our family. We call this "investing in our family." But what if inviting others in could actually build better families than we can on our own?

For many of us, this kind of investment means living near extended family. The idea of raising a family taking a village is seen through the eyes of extended family: They take care of you and you take care of them. Your community is your family. Grandma helps pick up the kids after school. Grandpa can go to the games you can't get to. This is a wider circle of community. Now it's not just "us four and no more." The circle might be eight or ten family members.

Jesus grew up in this type of community. In fact, it's the reason He went missing when He was twelve and no one noticed. It's a rather amusing story. Jesus travels to Jerusalem with His parents to visit the temple. They stay for a few days and begin the journey home. A couple of days into the trip, Mary and Joseph have a rather frightening and embarrassing conversation: "Have you seen Jesus lately?" "No, I thought He was with you!" "I thought He was with *you!*"

Can you imagine losing the Lord? I always thought this was particularly humorous—how do you misplace Jesus? But when I was in Israel I learned more about the path they would have traveled and the way they journeyed. Back then, pilgrims traveled in large groups. The women went first, then the children, and then the men. This was the safest way to commute in a region known for vandals. Hundreds of them made their way to Jerusalem this way. So it would make sense that if Joseph hadn't seen Jesus for a while, he would assume He was with the other kids or with His mom. And Mary would have figured Jesus was either with the kids or with His dad. In this case, the mass of community had its drawbacks, but the positive far outweighed the negative.

It was easier to live in community back then, before cars and planes and all the demands of a global society. Most of us today are more likely to travel farther from our birthplace and family of origin than in years past. Thankfully we can stay somewhat connected through technology. But what happens when we realize we need more than just an image on a screen?

The Benefits of a Wider Community

Lorrie and I were married for eight years before we had children. During those years we enjoyed multiple friendships, fun weekend getaways, and the freedom of not having to cart around a Pack 'n Play or a car seat. Community for us was rather fluid. A small group here, a ministry team there, or getting together with friends from work.

But when our first daughter was born, we realized how difficult being away from family could actually be. To see our parents meant a ten-hour drive for them. When the initial visit was over and they went home, we relished the downtime with our newborn, but then began to feel rather isolated. A date night would be good, but who would watch our baby? When Lorrie went back to work, a grandparent would have been handy. It was at this moment that we started thinking, *We actually do need a circle of community wider than our immediate family.*

Fortunately for us, we knew some sweet people next door who were retired. They loved our daughter and were very supportive, offering to help us out. We had them over for breakfast one Saturday morning and popped the question: "Would you be willing to watch Lindsey for a few hours a day?" They were delighted with the idea. But not half as much as we were! This would allow both Lorrie and me to return to work. Having them invest in us like this was a tremendous blessing. We knew

Lindsey would be in a loving environment. But to be honest, this was not real community. This was finding someone to bail us out.

For many of us, community means finding people to make our lives easier and better. I need a sitter. I need friends with kids my kids' ages for playdates. I need some other adults in my life for MY sanity. But the idea of community goes both ways.

The Mutual Benefits of Community

Sometimes we need others in our lives for *their* sake. And yes, we are still blessed as we minister to their needs. The reason Jesus' family lived in community wasn't just because they had no planes, trains, or automobiles. It was because of what God had decreed for them via Moses. In the sixth chapter of Deuteronomy (verse 5), we find the oft-quoted passage instructing us to "Love the LORD your God with all your heart, all your soul, and all your strength."

It's the passage displayed on Hobby Lobby art and hung in many Christian homes. We know the admonition to communicate this to our kids when we sit, walk, lie down, and rise up. We know we need to make sure this is part of their vernacular, mission statement, and training. But we often miss the intended *target* of the message. Moses did not give this instruction to every individual home and Christian cul-de-sac within earshot. Moses is addressing ALL of Israel, not just individual families.

Reggie Joiner and Carey Nieuwhof point this out in their fantastic book *Parenting Beyond Your Capacity*:

> Moses is speaking to all of Israel about the importance of families passing on their faith to the next generation. He was talking to every parent AND everyone else. We assume because there is

so much language about family and children that he was talking primarily to parents, but Moses was speaking to ALL of Israel. The culture of the Israelites was that of community. Not only were parents listening, but there were others in the crowd as well: aunts, uncles, grandparents, and a wider circle of adults.[1]

There's a need for us to "widen the circle," as this book suggests. The more voices you have in your children's lives saying the same things you are—the more likely they are to hear it. In fact, as I recall, the Barna Research Group has said that teens that have at least one adult from church make a significant time investment in their lives are more likely to keep attending church. I've found that when my kids' teachers and coaches say the same thing to them that I've been saying for years, my kids are more likely to heed the advice.

Stranger Danger

Now, we all know the pushback: "I'm not sure how well I know these people." After all, we are living in a different age than when our parents were young, and certainly when Jesus was young. Many people have faced trauma from family members or other people they thought they could trust. We hear the horror stories of children who suffered physical or psychological abuse at the hands of those who should have been protecting them. Such stories involve clergy at Protestant churches as well as Roman Catholic parishes.

We also hear of abuse by law enforcement officers, teachers, and coaches. Whether you were the victim or just know of victims, it can cause all of us to be overprotective when it comes to our kids. The thought of expanding the influencers on our family sounds appealing, but it feels unrealistic considering all the potential threats. Perhaps it might seem too big of a risk to take, but don't forget the other side of the coin: the great value to your family that comes from sharing your life with others.

Benefits of Serving Others

It's amazing how much serving others can benefit both the server and the one being served. Encouraging my kids to think of others is always a good choice. I remember my mother taking our young girls to the mall one year during Christmastime. The girls were especially excited because Grandma had given each of them a five-dollar bill.

They no doubt drove off with visions of the toys they might buy, but as they walked toward the mall they saw a Salvation Army bell ringer next to a collection bucket. As they walked by, Lindsey stopped and, to everyone's amazement, put her five-dollar bill in the bucket. Her sudden act of generosity awed my mother. Turning to her other granddaughter, she asked, "Sid, did you want to put something in?" Sidney replied, "I'm good." I guess 50 percent is better than nothing.

This type of influence forces our kids to think about more than themselves. We took our kids on a mission trip to Mexico one time, partly to serve but also to help them never to complain about having an iPhone that's three generations old. Spending a day with people who live in houses with dirt floors and playing with children who have broken toys and dilapidated bikes was a humbling experience for our whole family. My kids were broken up by this and left the next day with tears in their eyes. Influence is more than just sitting in a living room with others. Often it's going outside of our comfort zone to where others live.

One time stands out in particular. We made a trip to Orlando, Florida, to spend a few days with a church congregation we helped get started. I got to speak on the weekend and then we took the next couple of days as a family to enjoy Orlando. I say "enjoy" loosely, since it was the middle of July and the humidity was 110 percent. That being said, we decided to go to Universal Studios.

Yes, we do have Universal Studios in California, but why just have heat when you can have heat and humidity? Apparently we were not alone in wanting to visit this park. It appeared everyone in the state of Florida had also decided to go that day. The only thing worse than the heat and humidity, and the crowds, were the prices. I recognize we all need to eat and drink, but taking out a second mortgage on your home for lunch is not my preference.

After standing in two lines for two rides for two hours, I was ready for a break. My wife suggested we sit down in an actual restaurant and enjoy an air-conditioned lunch. It sounded like a good idea. As we got seated and received the menus, the kids began to look at the pictures on the menu while I stared at the prices. Just as I'd expected—for the price of this burger I should get the entire cow. It was at this point that my wife said, "Hey, why don't we pay for someone's lunch anonymously."

My kids of course agreed; they weren't springing for it. I was trying to find a polite way to say, "Maybe we can do that next time we are at McDonald's." But by now this selfless act was gaining momentum and the three of them were ganging up on me. The word *Scrooge* might have been considered. So I said, "Okay, there's a guy sitting by himself over there . . ." but before I could even finish the sentence, my wife said, "How about them?"

A mother and her daughter sat by themselves and appeared to be finishing up their meal. So when our server came back, we let her know of our intention and asked if she would keep it to herself. "Of course!" A few moments later she came over and said, "They asked for their bill and I told them someone had taken care of it. They were both stunned, and the mother began to tear up. They said to tell whoever it was 'Thank you so much!'"

The impact on my kids was immediate. They were so excited by this seemingly small gesture. And something strange happened as a result of that—it changed the tenor of our day. The generosity was contagious. We found ourselves waiting in line more patiently. It was easier and even fun to let people go in front of us from time to time. Even *I* was more relaxed. I stopped racing around the park cutting others off. I even let others cut me off without giving them the sigh and stare!

One act of generosity changed the rest of the day not just for that woman and her daughter but also for all of us.

The Value of Other Voices

A few years ago, my wife and I met another couple at our church that had a similar story to ours. Both of us had kids the same ages and we even had lived in some of the same places across the country. Kevin and Michelle had lived in Kentucky when we were there, and Michelle and Lorrie had known each other briefly at a school where they both taught. They'd just moved to our area, so my wife suggested we have them over for dinner. "Of course," I said. They came over and we had a great evening.

A few months later my wife said, "Let's have Kevin and Michelle over again." "Well, okay, that sounds fine." We did and it was great. Then they had us over to their house a week later. The following week, my introverted wife did something highly unusual—she invited them over *again*. I secretly wondered, *Who is this woman?*

"Okay," I agreed, "but shouldn't we spread the love a bit? Invite others over too, so Kevin and Michelle can get to know more people?" She said, "Sure, but we're never going to build deep lifelong friendships—the kind of friendships where our kids bond and other adults can speak into their lives—unless we put in the time."

She was right. So we began a tradition of every Friday night convening with this couple at either their house or ours. Nothing fancy, just food and conversation while the kids played. We'd catch up on the week, laugh about embarrassing moments, occasionally complain about issues at school, and often the kids would stay over with each other for the night.

Sometimes we'd even go out to eat and leave the kids at home with a sitter. Occasionally we'd vacation together. We made the investment of time, and slowly we began to see the results. I remember having a conversation with them over a slice of pie at a local restaurant. I said, "Would you be willing to be another voice for our kids?" "Oh, of course," they said. Then I followed that up with "I'm not sure if I said that right. Would you be willing to give advice, to even correct them, and to encourage them when you think it's necessary? Would you do that for our kids as well as your own?"

Suddenly this was sounding more like "We're setting up our will . . . can we put you down to take our kids if we die?" But they didn't bat an eye. "Of course. Will you do the same for us?" "Absolutely," I replied.

Over the next few years I remember many times Lorrie and I were able to attend their kids' activities and offer praise and encouragement. I think of conversations we were able to have with their kids as we took them home. And there were many times they would share words of encouragement and offer prayers up for our kids as well.

On one occasion I know how much it was needed. Our eight-year-old and their eight-year-old were the best of friends. And it just so happened that we had been told they were going to be in the same classroom in the upcoming school year. Nothing could be better! We were so thrilled, as was our daughter. But when we got to the school on the first day, we learned we were mistaken. They were not in the same class. This was devastating for our little girl. We consoled her as much as possible, but what really helped was when Michelle and Kevin began to offer their encouragement. "This is going to be a great year for you!"

There it was. I was seeing the positive influence of others being in our kids' lives. It was so much better than only having their parents on their support team.

How to Be Together . . . Better

Add chairs to the table

Anytime company comes, we add more chairs around the dining room table. Sometimes we need a bench, sometimes we need to straddle a table leg, but we fit people around it. It's important to all sit together. We all need to add more chairs to our family table. The influence on our kids and from our families must be expanded.

As busy as your schedule is, as crazy as your season of life might be, you need to find ways to bring others into your family's focus. It might be building friendships with neighbors who share your values or people in your church who can help communicate with your kids. It might be fostering kids or even adopting a grandparent at a senior center. However you do it, the circle must be expanded.

Like most churches, our church offers home Bible studies during the week. We call them Life Groups. People meet in homes to discuss the weekend message, have some dessert, and plan out ways to serve in the community. Lorrie and I started a group with our friends Kevin and Michelle and invited some other neighbors and new friends from the church to join us. Soon after this, our church sent us some other families who were looking for a group. So we gladly took them in.

One of these couples had a daughter the same age as our oldest daughter. We learned that while the mother and daughter were both believers, the dad was still holding back. He had some unanswered questions and some bad church experiences in his past, but they joined our group despite his hesitation.

We decided to bring our girls up to speed on what was going on. We told them Michael was not a Christian yet. Our girls loved the idea of praying for him every night. Fortunately, our oldest daughter and their daughter really hit it off. They would attend church events and school together and even had sleepovers from time to time.

Through their relationship and our Life Group, Michael stayed connected. He asked some questions here and there, but it was seeing people in the group living out their faith that he found most compelling. He continued to attend church and small group. His daughter made sure they never missed.

After a year of our doing life together, I decided to ask Michael a big question. We were two weeks away from our church's baptism weekend, so I sent him an email. "Michael, we are going to be doing baptisms on Super Bowl Sunday, and I was wondering if you might be ready to take that step? Are you ready to make that commitment?"

He wrote back: "I was actually just thinking the same thing." Baptizing Michael on Super Bowl Sunday was one of the highlights of my life. I so loved being a part of that, but even more than my excitement was our kids' excitement. Our daughters were seeing their prayers answered, and their friend's dad was making her the happiest girl in the world.

Engage the surrounding mission field

My kids need to see this kind of community at work. We live in California with lots of great things for them to do, but it is still far away from grandparents and cousins. It's a small circle we live in, so we need to widen it, not only for the sake of Christian community but also for the sake of being a light *in* the broader community. I want my kids to have a mission field mentality, so we regularly invite friends over who are not Christians. Our kids play with neighborhood kids who have no interest in God, and then invite them to church events.

It's a lot easier for them to invite someone and get a yes than it is for me. Everyone thinks my asking is self-serving, but they don't see the kids that way. So when we have a block party and my kids hear language they aren't accustomed to, or see alcohol flow like water, they aren't scared or bothered, because they are on a mission. And they love people who have different lifestyles just as much as they do anyone else.

An old oak tree used to stand outside our church in a neighboring parking lot. These trees are endangered here in California, so they are protected at all costs. When construction began on our building and the neighboring buildings, a fence was put around the giant tree to protect it. Lights were installed to highlight its grandeur through the night. Cars would drive by day and night and marvel at this massive tree. People wondered how it had stood the test of time for so many years. It looked impressive. Until it didn't.

One morning when we came to work, we noticed the giant old oak had collapsed during the night. It was later discovered that it had rotted from the inside out. All those years of watering, the fences and lights, and all the while it was decaying. I fear our families are sometimes bastions of protection too. We have our gated communities, closed garage doors, eight-foot-high fences, and self-focused approach to raising kids. But all the while we could be decaying from the inside out.

Discussion Questions

1. How is community different from family?
2. How can family serve as community in an effective way?
3. How large would you say your "circle" is now on a scale of 1 to 10?
4. What do you think it is about getting outside our comfort zone that can change our perspective so much?
5. What are some other things that we can do to practice being "better together" and widening our circle?

Impossible goals
are achieved together

I arrived in Dallas for a conference and immediately made my way to the rental car. There are always a variety of things you have to do when you get in a different car than the one you're used to. You may adjust the mirrors, the seat, maybe even the steering wheel, but for me, one of the first orders of business is to set the radio. Keep in mind this was a few years ago when not every car had Bluetooth or a USB connection to hook up your iPhone for personalized tunes. So I was faced with the task of trying to find a radio station I liked in an unfamiliar city.

I realize these are First-World problems, but it was an issue for me nonetheless. Once I found a good song, I began to drive. But the next song was not to my liking. So I hit the seek button. Finally I found something that wasn't Celine Dion or Waylon Jennings. But after that song, I was seeking, tuning, and scanning again.

This went on for three days. I nearly wrecked the car a few times. The struggle was real. I never found a station that was "me."

When I returned the car to the rental car facility, I walked up to the counter, handed in the paperwork and the keys, and turned to leave. That's when the attendant asked, "How'd you like the satellite radio?" "Excuse me?" I said in shock. He continued, "All our cars have Sirius XM radio—240 stations. How'd that work out for you?"

I was in disbelief. *You mean I could have been listening to Hair Nation for the past three days instead of constantly scanning the dial?* I thanked him for the tip, but encouraged him to lead with that next time. I had been driving around Dallas with an incredible gift and didn't even know it.

The gift of community seems to be that way for me. I often travel through my days focused on a mission, a goal, a destination, even an errand, and I don't even realize that others might not only help me get there quicker, but even bring more joy along the way. I know I'm not alone with this tendency. It's like we are Matthew McConaughey, driving around in the Lincoln talking to ourselves, while other people are all around us.

We have a woman on our staff who has lived this out for me. I got to know her years ago when I had the privilege of officiating at her wedding. Since then, she's become one of our most trusted volunteers. I always knew her to be a competent, resourceful, and dedicated volunteer, so when she asked if she could start serving in the office, I didn't hesitate. For a few years she sat in our office filing, stapling, answering calls, and helping with various clerical tasks. At the time, I had no idea how underutilized she was. She had come from the medical field, where she had managed an office filled with doctors. Can you imagine how difficult that must be? It's hard enough to read their writing! While she sat in our church office and shuffled papers, I was trying to manage a schedule, meetings, projects, and tasks (not wanting to overwhelm my assistant, who was also managing accounts receivable, payroll, and office politics).

One day someone suggested that I ask Debbie for some help. But something inside me said, "No, I got it." Why is it that we all struggle to release control? It might have something to do with pride.

Sometimes the Need Is Obvious

There are obviously times when we realize we need the help of others. No pregnant woman in labor willingly says, "I got this." No man stuck under a bench press of too much weight says, "I'll figure it out." With some tasks we welcome extra hands. But too often we think the task is well within our reach, so we don't look around for help.

But is the size of the task the real issue? Why are we reluctant to ask for help? Why do we always tell ourselves we can handle it—there's no need to bother anyone else? It doesn't matter what the task is. It might be coaching your son's Little League team or helping in your daughter's classroom. Maybe it's a project at work or something as simple as moving furniture.

Like many other people in America I fell prey to buying a treadmill. I made all the usual promises to myself: "It's cheaper than a gym membership." "This is perfect for the winter months when I can't run outside." I was sure I would use it more if it was in my home as opposed to across town at the gym. But— you guessed it—it eventually became a place to hang laundry. It didn't matter what room I put it in—the bedroom, living room, garage—the results were the same. Even if it were in front of the fridge or had a TV on it, I don't think it would have attracted me.

So it finally happened. We sold the treadmill to someone else who had the aspirations we once did. The only problem was, I had to get the beast (it was an older model and very heavy) downstairs. I watched three men carry it upstairs when we moved in, but I was convinced that with the help of gravity and my cunning ingenuity I'd be able to get it down the stairs on my own.

My wife kept offering reassuring suggestions like "Want me and the kids to help?" or "Why don't you call the neighbors?" But something in me said, "I can do this on my own. I don't need any help."

Pushing it to the stairs was exhausting enough. I tried using some carts—they broke. I tried blankets to drag it—they helped, but it kept swinging into the walls and doorframes. Finally I got it to the stairs. I thought, *It's all downhill from here. This will be the easy part.* I was partly right. It *was* all downhill. I began to push it down the stairs—one at a time. Then I had the bright idea to go to the bottom of the stairs and pull it toward me. As it began to slide, it hit every part of each wall, tearing the carpet and scraping up the banister in the process. Eventually I noticed it was picking up speed. Before I could react, I was pinned beneath it, and if not for getting hooked on the banister (and the grace of God) it would have run right over me.

Flat Stanley[1] comes to mind. The good news is it eventually got downstairs. The bad news? I had a lot of work ahead of me to patch up all the damage it left in its wake. Why is it that when the seemingly impossible lies ahead, we think, *I got this?*

I believe my behavior has served as motivation for our youngest daughter. Sidney is a driven and focused girl with high aspirations. She'll stop at nothing to attain them. In many cases that's a good thing, but it means sometimes she won't ask for help.

One day Sidney got the idea she'd redecorate the clubhouse I'd built for them in the backyard. She gave us strict instructions not to come outside or even look out till she was done. I think she didn't want to hear us say, "No, you can't do that," but mostly she wanted to do it on her own so she could wow us with the end result. I blame this on too much HGTV rather than on my example.

So we sat in the house while we heard a great deal of grunting, struggling, and nailing. Work was being done. Finally, my oldest daughter had had enough. She peeked out the window and turned to us in shock: "She's moving the futon into the clubhouse!"

Here's what you need to know about the futon. Though it was not as heavy as a sleeper couch, it was still a big item. It was being stored in our garage to be sold, and Sidney had navigated it out of the side garage door, through the backyard, and into the clubhouse. A ten-year-old! When we got out there for the grand reveal, she was sweating and exhausted, but she had done it. We marveled at her work, but wondered why she didn't ask for help. For the same reason I don't, and the same reason you don't.

Why We Don't Ask for Help

You might tell me I can't do it

There's nothing worse in our minds than to be halfway through a project only to hear, "Oh, that won't work." I'd actually rather complete it and fail than to hear you tell me it will never work. Even if you've already experienced it and know for a fact that it won't work, I still have this thought in my mind that I might somehow be the outlier. I think, *Maybe you didn't try it my way.* Sometimes I get it right, but most of the time I learn what you tried to tell me . . . that I can't do it that way.

King Solomon said, "Plans go wrong for lack of advice; many advisers bring success" (Proverbs 15:22).

Despite this sage advice from the wisest man who ever lived, I still go with Frank Sinatra and do things "my way."

You might tell me I shouldn't do it

The reason Sidney didn't tell us her plans for the clubhouse renovation was because even though we'd probably give permission, the permission would lack enthusiasm. She knew we'd probably say something like "Oh, don't do that." Or "That's a lot of work; wouldn't you rather do something else?" She was fixated on doing that particular task.

Don't we often avoid "many advisers" because someone in the group is bound to lack the vision we have? Someone will likely say, "Oh, you shouldn't do that." "I'm sure there's an easier way." "That may be more trouble than it's worth." So we either don't do it or we do it alone.

You might not do it the way I would

Not long ago I decided to put some cabinets in my church office. I was so proud of myself for conceptualizing the idea, gathering the measurements, picking out the proper cabinets at Lowes, and getting them into the truck by myself. When I hauled them into the church, several people stopped me and asked, "You need some help?" "No, I got it." And not like a martyr, but like a cowboy. I may have even acted like I was spitting tobacco. I was tough enough to handle this job on my own.

Later, as I returned to Lowes for more parts (because you never make just one trip to Lowes), I saw a poor fellow trying to load stuff in his truck while propping open the camper window with a two-by-four. It looked like quite an undertaking for one person, so I kindly offered, "You need a hand?" To which he said, "No, I got it." I walked off and started to laugh to myself about his ridiculous independence, only to remember what I'd said just an hour ago.

Why do I insist on doing it on my own? Because you may not do it the way I want you to. I have the vision. I have the plan. And I'd rather not have to explain it to you. It's easier to do it myself than to teach you how to do it.

You might get some of the credit

This one is hard to admit, but it's deep within us. If I share the workload, then I have to share the credit with you. Sometimes that's nice if you need someone to blame—like "The turkey came out dry." "Oh, well, Martha and I wondered how long to bake it." Now you've got a partner in crime.

But most of the time we think it's going to be successful and we want to revel in the potential compliments: "I've never had a meal this good!" "This is the best presentation to date." "No one fixes things as well as you." Though we don't like to admit it, many times we avoid many hands making light work for fear someone else will make the compliments light as well.

With all of these concerns about utilizing others' help to accomplish tasks in our life, it's easy to see why we waste our years on menial tasks and endless errands—things we can accomplish alone. To-do lists get checked, we feel like we're accomplishing things, but at the end of the day we realize all we really did was clear our email in-box. We know there's more than that to life. And deep down we have convictions that make us want to do more. But we are so shortsighted because we can only visualize the tasks that we can accomplish without the help of others.

In many ways we're addicted to inspiration and conviction, but not to change. We love movies, messages, and podcasts that tell us stories of global impact and cultural change, but that's what *others* do. There's no way we could. Most of us live vicariously through others. We read stories on social media of people losing weight, getting their degree, going on a mission trip, or starting a company, and we think, *I wish I was doing that*. We have a list of dreams we'd love to accomplish, but how can we find time for them? Perhaps many hands could make our dreams a lighter load to handle. And what looks impossible could actually be achieved.

In the Old Testament there's a story of a guy named Nehemiah. Though he was living in another country, his home was back in Israel. His people were in Jerusalem. And when he learned they were leaderless and without protection or direction, his heart broke. Nehemiah's story teaches us that *what* gets done is more important than *who* gets it done. When we shift our thinking this way, we can accomplish the impossible. Nehemiah struggled with the same obstacles we do in believing *together is better*.

To understand Nehemiah's story, we have to scroll back to the year 600 BC. This is when the Babylonians came in and conquered Israel and took all their young men away to serve King Nebuchadnezzar. Within the next seventy years the nation of Israel pretty much shut down. Their future had been carried away to Babylon.

Then the Persians conquered the Babylonians. The Persian king, Cyrus the Great, decided there was no longer any need for the exiled Jews to be there so he told them to go home. Slowly they trickled back to Israel, but it didn't go so well. They'd been gone too long. What was left of Israel was in ruins, Jerusalem was a disaster, and people from other cultures had moved in and settled in the Jewish homeland. Enter Nehemiah, about ninety years after the decree to go home had been issued.

Although Nehemiah was a Jewish man by heritage, we don't know if he'd ever been to Israel or Jerusalem. For some reason his ancestors, when given the chance to return to Israel, decided to stay put. So when we meet Nehemiah, he has been raised in Persia and is now working for King Artaxerxes.

In many ways, Nehemiah has it good in Persia. He's in the service of the king and living in the palace. He has a steady job. In his mind, he assumes everything back in Jerusalem is good. After all, the exile ended ninety years ago. Then one day some relatives return from visiting Israel and Nehemiah asks, "How's everything back in the mother land?" His brothers begin to unpack details for him of trouble and disgrace. The place is in shambles, the gates have been burned, and the wall is broken down. They have no security, so neighboring countries are running all over them. Here's Nehemiah's reaction: "When I heard these things, I sat down and wept. For some days I mourned and fasted and prayed before the God of heaven" (Nehemiah 1:4 NIV).

It is from this time with God that Nehemiah knows what to do. He is to head to Jerusalem and rebuild the wall. How? Who knows? But his mission is clear.

The Impossible Begins with Personal Mission

In many ways Nehemiah is living an enviable life in Persia. But much like fearing that others would get the credit or not do it his way, he takes on the task of rebuilding Jerusalem as his own mission. Seemingly, he's the only one who feels compelled to go. He's not joining a movement, he's starting one. And when you start one, it's hard to ask others to join.

But what Nehemiah's story teaches us is that even though the mission starts with you, it ends with others getting involved. This is not a secret mission. Nehemiah is not James Bond. God's vision comes to one but employs many.

The very first thing he has to do is go to the king and ask for time off: "Do you mind if I take a few months off, maybe years, to go home and build a wall?" Imagine turning in that request to Human Resources.

But Nehemiah doesn't stop there. He's bold enough to say, "Oh, and do you mind providing protection for me on my journey?" "You got it, Nehemiah," the king seems to respond. Just as Nehemiah is about to walk out the door he thinks, *What do I have to lose?* So he says to the king, "Oh, and will you provide me the wood I need to build the wall?" Talk about pushing your luck. But Nehemiah is proving something to us—while impossible dreams may be given to individuals, making them a reality is realized together.

Here's where we often get stuck. We can ask for money and input, but then we want to take it from there. It's sometimes easier to ask for money for the church project than it is to let others help us accomplish it. Nehemiah had secured the king's money and resources. No doubt he felt the pressure we all feel—the juice better be worth the squeeze!

Once we get this far it's natural to think, *I better take it from here.* After all, they've put their trust in me. They bought *my* vision, not our vision. I better make it worth their while. But Nehemiah will prove for us there's a better way.

The Impossible Continues with a Team

After Nehemiah arrives at the wall, he spends an entire evening touring the site. He sees all the holes, the wreckage, and the debris. He's overwhelmed with what needs to be done, and though he feels the pressure to do it right, since the king's resources are backing him, he knows this is not a one-man job. He turns to all the remnant of Israel living there, saying:

> You see the trouble we are in: Jerusalem lies in ruins, and its gates have been burned with fire. Come, let us rebuild the wall of Jerusalem, and we will no longer be in disgrace.
>
> Nehemiah 2:17 NIV

But he doesn't stop with his call to action. He also lets them in on his vision: "I also told them about the gracious hand of my God on me and what the king had said to me" (Nehemiah 2:18 NIV).

Nehemiah leans into others around him to help him and progress begins. Can you imagine the work ahead? Where do you start? He's never done this before. He doesn't know what to do. But he knows he's not alone. He has a team. And they have momentum. After all, who wouldn't want a wall?

Critics Are Inevitable

That's when the critics come out. We are introduced to two hecklers in Nehemiah's story named Sanballat and Tobiah. Isn't this always the case? Start doing something good and someone is sure to throw stones.

When we started planning a new church building, we had so much momentum. Everyone in the church loved the idea of our getting a permanent home. Finally, we would be moving out of the movie theater and high school stage of our lives and into our own building. The problem was that not everyone outside the church loved the idea. Neighbors petitioned the city for our project not to be approved. They spoke out about the noise and traffic we would bring to their neighborhood.

Once we made it past these problems and the building went up, they began to complain about how we'd built it. Some thought it wasn't nice enough—it doesn't even look like a church!—while others felt it was too extravagant. We were called a church of gimmicks, the church with cupholders, the church that's a mile wide and an inch deep.

As the lead pastor, I was criticized as someone "just in it for the money." On and on it went. When your dream is criticized, you feel the pressure. I wanted to run and hide. I wanted to quit. I wondered if I'd ever be able to trust anyone ever again. I wanted not only to succeed but also to prove my critics wrong.

Nehemiah had to have felt this. This was his dream, his mission. And it was from God. He wanted nothing but good for his people, and here came these critics who were making his life miserable. Then to top it off, neighboring countries were threatening to come in and wipe them all out before they finished the wall. It was another chance for Nehemiah to quit or retreat. But rather than take the threat personally, he took it seriously.

Refusing to Quit Brings the Unstoppable God

"From that day on, half of my men did the work, while the other half were equipped with spears, shields, bows and armor" (Nehemiah 4:16 NIV).

Half of the people stood in the gaps of the wall with spears, bows, and shields that held off any attacks while the rest just kept working. And look at what happens as a result:

Then I said to the nobles, the officials and the rest of the people, "The work is extensive and spread out, and we are widely separated from each other along the wall. Wherever you hear the sound of the trumpet, join us there. Our God will fight for us!"

Nehemiah 4:19–20 NIV

I love what Nehemiah highlights here: The work will spread us out . . . and it will separate us . . . but when we come to meet each other's needs, our God will fight for us.

And that's what they did. They built, protected, prayed, and completed the wall in an astounding fifty-two days. That's less than two months!

We truly are better together, because God is there and He is unstoppable.

How to Partner Together . . . Better

Let people in on your mission

Many of us can relate to Nehemiah. We have a dream or an idea. But we let critics, pressure, opinions, or fear cause us to hesitate. We often do this because we think we have to accomplish the impossible on our own.

Maybe for you it's quitting a habit, forgiving a parent, building a family, starting a business, going back to school, finishing your degree, or committing to restoring your marriage.

For me, it was building the new church structure. It seemed impossible. The critics were plentiful. I was under the watchful eye of donors who kept saying, "I wouldn't have done it that way."

But back to this amazing person in our office named Debbie. I sat down with her one day and said, "Do you think you can help me with a few things?" "Absolutely." So I gave her a few tasks, thinking I shouldn't load her up with too much. But one day she came to me and said, "You realize we all believe in this mission we're on. Let us help you! I can keep booking your flights and scheduling meetings, but I think there is more I can take off your plate." Essentially she was saying, "Trust us with the mission too." So I did.

This led to being able to trust others even more. I realized that I had a group of people around me on staff and on our board of directors who were willing and able to help . . . they just hadn't been given my permission.

I had to entrust them with our mission and my personal vision. I had to let them in on the pressure I felt and the criticism I had to handle. And what I learned was that in every instance where I wanted to *run from*, I decided to *run toward* community. We could achieve so much more if we did it together.

Was it easy? Of course not, but it was worth it. Let people in on your "impossible" dream. They just might help you achieve it.

Discussion Questions

1. Are you someone who works better with others or better alone? Why?

2. Do you find it hard to ask for help? Why or why not?

3. Despite our personalities, many times we don't realize other people can help us accomplish our goals faster. Why do we find this difficult? How can inviting others in to help actually speed up the process?

4. Why do you think we have such a hard time sharing ownership? How can we get better at this?

5. As we saw with Nehemiah, "rather than taking the threat personally, he took it seriously." In what ways can criticism be a source of motivation and team building?

6. What is the biggest "mission" in your life in which you need to be more inclusive of others and accept help?

Home is discovered together

When my youngest daughter, Sidney, was six she decided she was ready to be on her own. The rules at Prison George apparently were too strict, so she was going to take freedom into her own hands. I can't even recall what she was upset about. I do remember that we were still picking out her clothes for her at that age and she was much more particular than her older sister. I'm not saying her temper was out of control concerning fashion, but we may or may not have used the phrase *the devil wears Prada*.

Whatever the issue was, she threw a fit sufficient to be sent to her room. She stewed around in there as we stood outside her door wondering what to do next. Lorrie and I found that the "Go to your room" directive was more for us than for our kids. It allowed us time to strategize. "What should we do?" "I don't know. I was hoping you'd know!"

As a pastor I should know these things, right? But as I often tell people, the Bible is filled with a lot of bad parenting. Isaac blessed the wrong kid, Jacob told his sons that Joseph was his favorite, and Mary and Joseph left Jesus in Jerusalem and didn't realize it for three days!

Fortunately God redeemed all those things, so we prayed that God would redeem our family situation too. While we were plotting our next move, we noticed it grew quiet behind her door. The tantrum had ended. Was this the calm before the storm? It was at this point we saw a handwritten note sliding out from under the door. I was hoping for a letter of apology, but expected it to be a list of demands. Instead it read:

I am running away from home. You have been mean to me my whole life. I will miss you. Love, Sidney

The letter was sad, sweet, alarming, and a bit funny. She'd had six hard years and that was enough. But she would miss us. The best part was the P.S.

P.S. I'll be at the Youngs'.

The Youngs were neighbors of ours. I was thrilled she had a plan. I was elated it was with people we knew. But I was most touched by the sentiment behind the admission of revealing where she would be. "I'm running away from home, but here's where I'll be. Please come and get me!"

Sidney never left home, and the story has been with us ever since.

Her thoughts are our thoughts as well. We get mad at people, we get frustrated with our family, and our co-workers drive us crazy. But in most cases we beg them not to leave us alone. "Please come and get me."

It's been said that the fear that's worse than death is the fear of dying alone. We all want to be in a warm bed surrounded by loved ones as they help us exit this world into the next. We want others to help us reach home.

From This Life to the Next

Dallas Willard once said that since life is just a series of experiences, we may not even know we are dead until a while after we have passed. We'll just be having new experiences. He goes on to say that since life is a collection of experiences, the definition of intimacy is to share an experience. We want to share the experience of going home with others . . . until we can share the next experience with Jesus.[1]

Living a life "better together" is more than just a pursuit so we can cope with the reality of this life. It is also a method that allows us to get to our final destination—our eternal home in heaven.

In the letter to the Hebrews, the book we keep returning to, the author is concerned that his church may stray from the course. They've endured hardship and faced difficulty. Their faith has been challenged in ways most of us will never understand. Most of us will never lose our job, our family, or our freedom because of our faith. They did. Yet the author pushes them to something bigger.

Look at the words he uses:

Persevere
Don't shrink back
Hold the confidence we had at first firmly till the end
Enter in with confidence

Make every effort

Hold unswervingly to the hope we profess

The goal is more than day-to-day. It is a lifetime of faithful service and communion with the Lord and His body.

We understand this goal. We don't want our loved ones to "shrink back." We want our children to "persevere." But how do they (and we) do that all alone? How can we help others who are far from us? How do we "make every effort"?

Could it be that our clear-cut method, preventing us from backsliding or from wavering from the faith, is to do life together? Could it be that it's not enough to say, "It's just Jesus and me"?

Reaching Back

Chapter 11 of Hebrews highlights a long list of people who have gone on before us. These people had extraordinary faith and that faith motivated the next generation to keep their faith. This ripple effect carried on and on. From Abraham to Isaac to Jacob to Joseph, faith was able to overcome even in the lives of the most imperfect individuals. We are reminded of Moses and his parents, and the faith that helped them to brave the evil culture of their day, eventually enabling Moses to lead God's people out of slavery.

> Therefore, since we are surrounded by such a great cloud of witnesses, let us throw off everything that hinders and the sin that so easily entangles. And let us run with perseverance the race marked out for us.
>
> Hebrews 12:1 NIV

I used to think that the great cloud of witnesses was the world. The witnesses were those watching to see if we were truly followers of Jesus or just hypocrites. Now I see it differently. I believe the author is calling our attention to the grandstands of faithful people in heaven who are cheering us on.

When you feel alone, remember what David said when he was hiding from Saul: "I put my trust in you, God." When you are betrayed, remember Joseph who languished in a prison cell for a crime he didn't commit. When you feel like your best days are behind you, remember that old shepherd named Moses who went on to take down the great Egyptian Empire. Sometimes being *together* is remembering whose family you are in. We are all children of the same God. We all benefit from His presence. We all benefit from being a part of the same family of believers.

Reaching Forward

Toward the end of chapter 11, the author of Hebrews offers a somewhat strange observation. After listing names like Gideon, Barak, Samson, Jephthah, David, Samuel, and the prophets he makes this statement: "All these people earned a good reputation because of their faith, yet none of them received all that God had promised" (Hebrews 11:39).

Why was God's promise yet to be fulfilled for them? What's He waiting for? Isn't that what we all wonder as we wait for our heavenly home?

Maybe God isn't waiting at all. Have you considered that time itself came into being at creation? God stands outside of time, but He put boundaries around our existence, calling them day and night. If He can see everything at once, He sees beyond us and behind us. From His perspective there is no past and no future, as there is for us. And together the entire story makes sense, even when it doesn't make sense to us in the chapter we are living in.

My wife, Lorrie, was driving in downtown Los Angeles and got lost. My wife is wonderful, even if a bit directionally challenged. We can't be perfect, after all. Rather than using the on-screen navigation or even her phone apps, she called me to ask, "How do I get home?"

I quickly located her by using the location app on her phone, and from my vantage point I could see exactly where she was, where she was headed, and where she needed to be. I calmly directed her down the streets, to the freeway, and got her on the road leading home. It was easier for me because I could see the whole scene from above. She only saw the immediate, where she was at the moment.

For the people mentioned in Hebrews, God had something in mind and it involved other faithful followers of God: "For God had something better in mind for us, so that they would not reach perfection without us" (Hebrews 11:40).

How did believers in the first century AD have anything to do with Moses, or Rahab, or Enoch? It was something they'd all been a part of—the coming of Jesus. Through Jesus' death and resurrection the true fulfillment of all God's promises had been provided. Abraham was now the father of *many* nations. Moses' people could now be led out of *spiritual* slavery. And Rahab was now a relative of the King of Kings. Those who were martyred and tortured for their prophecies were now justified. What they had spoken of before it happened was now a reality.

Jesus and His kingdom *made sense* of all the directions God had been giving before He came. The strange twists and turns throughout the history of Israel and the world all led to Calvary.

Jesus' resurrection and the establishing of His kingdom now brought clarity to past events. It's similar to how (on a much smaller scale) I directed my wife home by means of what seemed to her strange turns and confusing streets. None of it made sense to her until she reached her destination.

Ultimately, God's way to save the world involved people . . . lots of people. It began with Abraham hearing from God that he would be the father of many nations and "blessed to be a blessing." (See Genesis 12:1–3.) As his nation grew they encountered slavery, exile, abandonment, genocide, and near extinction, but they remained a testimony to God's faithfulness.

From that remnant came Jesus, who ushered in the kingdom of God. In salvation it was never God's intention for us to see it as "just Jesus and me." Instead, God's intention was that His kingdom would be Jesus and His community of believers. His body, His church.

Just as the Son of God existed in community, we must live in community as well. Once the veil in the temple was torn in two, all of us were welcomed into this great rescue mission for the world called the kingdom of God. And we are all blessed— not just to pray for more blessings, not just to tweet pictures of ourselves on the beach and #blessed—but *to be a blessing*. As Paul said to the Ephesians: "God's purpose in all this was to use the church to display his wisdom in its rich variety to all the unseen rulers and authorities in the heavenly places" (Ephesians 3:10).

God is showing us that His kingdom will be made up of the most unique collection of ragamuffins and vagabonds imaginable. It will be led by the simple and upheld by the weak. It will be a band of misfits and broken vessels, but it will declare His wisdom and show off His genius and power.

Being better together will not only get us through the day-to-day challenges of life but will also take us home. We are united with the patriarchs and the heroes of the past as well as the missionaries, teachers, and leaders of the future. We are part of the kingdom of God. And embracing that fact makes us better together.

More than Jesus

John was a guy who only needed Jesus. He wanted Him as a rabbi. Back in Jesus' day, you didn't pick a school, you picked a teacher. And if they chose you, you would follow them, learn from them, become like them.

So when Jesus chose John to be one of His disciples, John was thrilled. Jesus chose twelve to follow Him and learn from Him. Among these twelve guys, there were three that Jesus was especially close to: Peter, James, and John. And among those three, Jesus loved John like a kid brother.

Everyone was thrilled to be along for the ride, but John eclipsed them all. He liked the other guys, but he focused his attention and devotion on Jesus. John witnessed all the miracles, heard all the teachings, was involved in all the campfire discussions, and went to church with Jesus for three years.

When He was preparing for the Last Supper, Jesus asked John to help get the room ready. When He went out to the garden to pray before being crucified, John was with Him. And when Jesus was arrested, John was there. He saw the flogging and witnessed the crucifixion. He was so close to the action that he stood by Jesus' mother at the foot of the cross and heard Jesus say, "John, take care of my mom." John experienced the agony of losing his best friend. All he ever wanted and needed was Jesus. Now He was gone.

Three days later John hears that He's alive. He runs to the tomb to look in—and sure enough, Jesus' body is not there. It wouldn't be long after this that John sees his Lord. They eat together. They spend weeks together. Everything will be fine now, he figures. Jesus is back, and all John needs is Jesus. But then he has to say good-bye to Him again. This time it was less painful, but still bittersweet. His Lord was leaving.

John will now dedicate the rest of his life to telling people about Jesus—traveling, teaching, healing, and writing. His message is clear: "All you need is Jesus." In the years after Jesus left, John and the other disciples recklessly spread the news about who Jesus was—God come to earth—and assured everyone that they could find new life in Him. The church grew and grew and grew. "All you need is Jesus."

At the time, the Roman government didn't care who met together or who worshiped what, as long as you declared that Caesar was Lord. But the church refused to do that. They declared Jesus as the King of Kings. The Romans let the Jews slide when it came to their loyalty because the Jewish religion predated them. At first, Christianity seemed to be enough like Judaism not to raise any suspicion, but eventually the Romans began to figure it out. This new upstart religion, which no longer identified with the Jewish one, was not loyal to Caesar as Lord. So it came under suspicion.

During this time a ruler named Nero arose. And you could say he was insane. He killed his own family members. He even tried to burn down Rome so he could rebuild the city in his honor. The Roman citizens weren't too happy about this, so Nero blamed the fire on the Christians, turning everyone against the growing group of Jesus followers.

Over the next few years, persecution broke out and Christians died in horrific ways. They were thrown to the lions, drawn and quartered, and even covered in tar, affixed to poles, lit on fire, and used to light Nero's parties at night.

It was during these persecutions that the other disciples lost their lives. John was boiled alive, rescued before death, and then exiled to the island of Patmos, forty miles off the coast of Turkey.

This is where he is at the beginning of his book called the Revelation. He's broken, tired, and alone, and he's got to be thinking, *Have I joined the losing team?*

We've all felt that way before. Start going to church and things seem to get worse. Start providing boundaries for your kids and they barrel over them. Begin to tithe and you lose your job. Recently I had coffee with a friend who said, "Four years ago I decided to get serious about my faith, and since that time I've had a steady decline in revenue at work." He concluded hopefully, stating it as a question, "I'm assuming God has a plan?"

John is alone. John is broken. But John is with Jesus!

I, John, your brother and companion in the suffering and kingdom and patient endurance that are ours in Jesus, was on the island of Patmos because of the word of God and the testimony of Jesus. On the Lord's Day I was in the Spirit, and I heard behind me a loud voice like a trumpet, which said: "Write on a scroll what you see and send it to the seven churches: to Ephesus, Smyrna, Pergamum, Thyatira, Sardis, Philadelphia and Laodicea." I turned around to see the voice that was speaking to me. And when I turned I saw seven golden lampstands, and among the lampstands was someone like a son of man, dressed in a robe reaching down to his feet and with a golden sash around his chest.

Revelation 1:9–13 NIV

Even in exile, John was still having a church service, even though the attendance was just one. But in the middle of this worship experience, the attendance grows to two . . . Jesus shows up.

What happens next is nothing short of amazing. Jesus will take John on a tour of heaven that will leave the church trying to make sense of it for the rest of the church age. But the first thing Jesus does is turn John's attention to the seven churches scattered across Asia Minor at this time.

We might wonder, *Why was it so important that John be shown what was happening in these churches? Wouldn't he rather see a tour of heaven, or just spend time with Jesus?* I know many Sundays I would prefer to attend Bedside Baptist. Or go play golf with Jesus. Yet this was first on the agenda for Him: to take John to church.

I'm sure John had questions he'd like to ask his Lord. "Where have you been? Why haven't you returned for your church yet? We've been waiting, you know. We've done all you said to do, so why are we being persecuted? We may be destroyed by Nero. We need you to sweep in and save the day!"

If nothing else, John would have had plenty to catch up on with his best friend. It had probably been thirty years since he'd seen his Lord and Master. John had been entrusted with the care of Jesus' mother. Wouldn't He want an update on that?

But Jesus doesn't even entertain those issues. He takes John to church. And in doing that, He highlights an important concept: "Yes, John, I AM enough. But you need the church too. You are better together."

So as John writes these seven letters to the seven churches, his mind will turn to them and he'll focus not on his own issues but on theirs. He will lift them up in prayer and process their pain. He will admonish them, challenge them, and even rebuke them. Something about this experience will lift John's spirits and cause him to not lose hope. Jesus knows that we need people to help us make it home.

What's fascinating to me is that John's gospel is written by John *after* his experience on the island. He is later released from this prison camp—probably due to old age—and it is then that he sits down to write his memoir of his time with Jesus—the gospel of John.

When he tells us about the Last Supper, he gives us more detail than any of the other gospel writers. While most condense the event to what equates to one chapter, John gives us five chapters about it. Nearly 25 percent of his gospel, in fact, is dedicated to that event. He even lets us know his place there—he's the one seated next to Jesus. But the thing that always brings a lump to my throat is how he describes himself. He's "the one Jesus loved" (John 20:2 NIV).

I could understand it if he'd written the account a few days after the event. He got to sit next to Jesus. They were close friends. He had been invited to see the transfiguration, pray with Jesus, and even take care of His mother. But this was written after *years* of persecution, years spent on a prison island away from everyone who loved him. This comes at the end of John's life, and he still feels loved by Jesus. He's "the one Jesus loved." I wonder if it has anything to do with Jesus' taking John to church.

It is the way chosen by Jesus to lead John home. And it's the way Jesus leads us home. *Together.*

How to Be Together . . . Better

Be like Jesus so others see Jesus till we meet Him

I remember the first time I met Sherry. She was sitting outside our church building waiting for the bus. She was a very unassuming woman who appeared to have seen hard times. Her clothes looked secondhand, her hair was thinning, and her eyes were glazed over from glaucoma. But her smile was so real and genuine, you could tell she knew Jesus.

We spoke briefly. She complimented me on my sermon that morning, and I thanked her for her kind words. But I would be seeing more of Sherry. She began faithfully serving on our prayer team. Many times I'd walk off the platform and she'd be sitting there behind it having prayed for me the entire time I was preaching. She also led a women's group. She'd find ways to meet with women and teach the Bible, letting them share their lives with her while she shared hers with them.

What I later learned was that Sherry lived by herself in a convalescent home. She was losing her eyesight. And she took the bus everywhere she went. Serving others and meeting with people might have seemed like a lot of hassle to some people, but in her mind it was a blessing. She was grateful to God for helping her break an addiction to alcohol and for the years she'd been given. Even when she was diagnosed with cancer, it didn't slow her down. She continued to serve and pray. I'd get notes and phone calls from her, sharing her prayers for the church and for me.

When her struggle with cancer hospitalized her, she was visited by one of our pastors. We worried this unassuming, quiet woman might be all alone. But when he asked for her room number, the receptionist said, "Follow the smell of flowers. It's been a steady stream of visitors, flowers, and cards to her room!" Apparently, even though Sherry was quiet and unassuming, she was also consistent, even heroic in her own way. And people recognized how her prayers had helped pull them through.

When Sherry finally went home to be with her Lord, people came from all over to honor her and tell her story. She was Jesus to others, she saw Jesus in others, and they held her hand until she met Jesus face-to-face.

The hope of heaven is often what we say will help us to stay the course in our faith. But as Jesus reminded John, as the author of Hebrews reminded his church, and as we are reminded throughout Scripture, we do not sojourn alone. We travel in our faith walk in community. And it is when we are Jesus to others that we see Jesus in them, and they see Jesus in us. One day we'll all meet Him together and then we'll know: We're better together.

Discussion Questions

1. How does the Dallas Willard quote change the way you see life? If life is a series of experiences, and you want to get the most out of it, how do you do that? How does this view affect the way you describe or think about heaven?

2. "Sometimes being together is remembering whose family you are in." Remembering who you are often involves *where* and *who* you've come from. Discuss.

3. What is so motivating about our living better together in the present so we can be an example or foundation for others in the future?

4. The author references the book of Revelation toward the end of this chapter. This can be a tough read for many people. However, how does the fact that it was a letter to real people in real churches change the way you read it? What impact does it have on us in the present?

Notes

Introduction: Taking a Selfie

1. From a message delivered at the Celebrate Recovery Summit, 2016, at Saddleback Church, Lake Forest, California.

2. For those who've never heard of this, it's coffee mixed with coconut oil and grass-fed-sourced unsalted butter.

Chapter 1: I don't need anyone

1. Frederick D. Bruner, *A Theology of the Holy Spirit* (Eugene, OR: Wipf & Stock Publishers, 1997).

2. An Extrovert is a person who is energized by people and drained by solitude. An Introvert is just the opposite. While Introverts may be able to successfully engage in social settings, they find them draining and need time alone to recharge. An Influencer is someone who enjoys forwarding a cause or value by leveraging relationships. And they do so while thinking relationship first, results second. A Driver, on the other hand, thinks results first and then relationships if needed. For them, the end always justifies the means.

Chapter 2: No one "gets" me

1. For more information, see www.strengthsfinder.com/home; www.disc profile.com/what-is-disc/overview; www.5lovelanguages.com.

2. https://www.theguardian.com/stage/2005/Sep/29/comedy.religion

3. Larry Osborne, *Innovation's Dirty Little Secret* (Grand Rapids, MI: Zondervan, 2013), 37.

4. Max Lucado, *In the Grip of Grace* (Nashville: Thomas Nelson, 1996), chap. 16.

Chapter 4: Intimacy with God is deeper together

1. Ichak Adizes, *Managing Corporate Lifecycles Vol. 2* (Santa Barbara, CA: Adizes Institute Publications, 2015), chap. 1.
2. Shared at Real Life Church, Valencia, California, August 2013.
3. Brennan Manning, *The Rabbi's Heartbeat* (Colorado Springs: Nav-Press, 2003), 123.

Chapter 5: Joy is found quicker together

1. Eugene Peterson, *A Long Obedience in the Same Direction* (Downers Grove, IL: InterVarsity Press, 1980), 96–97.

Chapter 6: Anxiety is calmed together

1. I attribute this to seeing just the preview for a movie called *Magic*, where a talking doll comes to life. What pushed me over the edge was when I was in my neighbor's basement and saw one of those dolls on the shelf. I never went in there again.
2. Larry Osborne, *Accidental Pharisees* (Grand Rapids, MI: Zondervan, 2012), 20.
3. James B. Smith, *Embracing the Love of God* (New York: HarperCollins, 2010), e-book.

Chapter 7: Healing happens together

1. Malcolm Gladwell, *Outliers* (New York: Little, Brown, and Co., 2008).
2. Robert Putnam, *Bowling Alone* (New York: Simon & Schuster, 2000).
3. C. S. Lewis, *Surprised by Joy* (Boston: Houghton Mifflin Harcourt, 1955), 266.
4. Shane Claiborne, *Common Prayer: A Liturgy for Ordinary Radicals* (Grand Rapids: Zondervan, 2010), 137.
5. Jean Vanier in Claiborne, *Common Prayer*, 163.
6. John Ortberg, *Everybody's Normal Till You Get to Know Them* (Grand Rapids, MI: Zondervan, 2003), 44.
7. Brené Brown, *The Gifts of Imperfection* (Center City, MN: Hazelden, 2010), 6.
8. Quoted in Smith, *Embracing the Love of God*.

Chapter 8: Temptations are conquered together

1. Smith, *Embracing the Love of God*, 63–64; 35.
2. John Ortberg, *Soul Keeping* (Grand Rapids, MI: Zondervan, 2014), 150.

Chapter 9: Perfectionists find peace together

1. This song is from the 1930s, revived in the 1960s when Joan Baez sang it on tour. The word means "Come by here" in Gullah, a creole dialect of former slaves living off the South Carolina and Georgia coast.

Chapter 10: Families are built to last together

1. Reggie Joiner and Carey Nieuwhof, *Parenting Beyond Your Capacity* (Colorado Springs: David C. Cook, 2010), 64.

Chapter 11: Impossible goals are achieved together

1. The character from the children's book *Flat Stanley* by Jeff Brown.

Chapter 12: Home is discovered together

1. Dallas Willard in John Ortberg, *Soul Keeping*, 188.

Rusty George is the lead pastor of Real Life Church (RLC) in Valencia, California. Over his fifteen years at RLC, the church has grown to more than 6,000 people and three campuses. Rusty speaks regularly at conferences across the country, and he lives with his wife and two daughters in Santa Clarita, California.